The Big Book of Business Quotes

The Big Book
of Business Quotes

OVER 1,400 OF THE SMARTEST THINGS EVER SAID
ABOUT MAKING MONEY

EDITED BY JOHNNIE L. ROBERTS

Skyhorse Publishing

Skyhorse Publishing books may be purchased in bulk at special discounts for sales promotion, corporate gifts, fund-raising, or educational purposes. Special editions can also be created to specifications. For details, contact the Special Sales Department, Skyhorse Publishing, 307 West 36th Street, 11th Floor, New York, NY 10018 or info@skyhorsepublishing.com.

Skyhorse˙ and Skyhorse Publishing˙ are registered trademarks of Skyhorse Publishing, Inc.˙, a Delaware corporation.

Visit our website at www.skyhorsepublishing.com.

10 9 8 7 6 5 4 3 2 1

Library of Congress Cataloging-in-Publication Data is available on file.

Cover design by Rain Saukas

Print ISBN: 978-1-5107-7112-3
Ebook ISBN: 978-1-63450-021-0

Printed in the United States of America

Previously published as *The Big Book of Business Quotations*
(ISBN: 978-1-63220-591-9).

To my anchors:
Wife Adrienne, daughters Lily and Ava,
and mother Susie Jackson.

Table of Contents

Introduction

The *Wall Street Journal*, which was first published on July 8, 1889, is one of the oldest and most famous publications devoted to daily reporting on business, finance, and the economy. It also is arguably the world's most authoritative source on the art of the business quote. Having reported for the *Journal* for fifteen years, I have firsthand knowledge of the deep wisdom about and reverence for the business quotes inside that august daily business newspaper. And because I share that reverence, I was honored to compile *The Big Book of Business Quotes*.

Until I joined the *Journal*'s reporting staff in 1981, I couldn't have imagined that business quotes were viewed as a kind of literary gemstone. Nor had I realized that business quotes were so widely coveted. Writers, thinkers, businesspeople, speechwriters, sloganeers, essayists, spiritualists, executive coaches, a broad cross-section of civic leaders, clergy, lawyers, students, and carnival barkers alike all find need at one time or another to brandish a business quote.

Like all gemstones, however, business quotes vary widely in quality. As a result, the quotes in these pages made the cut only after the most discriminating consideration. Predictable utterances—"If at first you don't succeed, try again"—were routinely banished. I evaluated the sharpness and forcefulness of the quotes and included a wide range of voices and authors. I provided the source of the quotes where possible, though the true origin of many is unknown. Quotes from unknown sources had to be unusually incisive or insightful to be included.

The quotes that follow provoke deep thought, buttress credibility, convey scope, and even tug on emotions. I hope they spark your creativity and prove to be useful in your endeavors.

Advertising

Among the many ruins of Pompeii were dainty perfume bottles, a statuette of Alexander the Great, and, of course, advertising. The *New World Encyclopedia*, in fact, informs us that the origins of "commercial" messaging is prehistoric, and advertising was among the earliest forms of human communication. While civilizations have come and gone, the prevalence of come-ons to consumers is ubiquitous. GroupM, the global media investment group, says that nearly $1 trillion a year (as of 2016) is poured into drawing consumers' attention worldwide, prompting their purchase of goods and services. And advertising has advanced toward the realm of science fiction. Advertisers can now target and geographically trail mobile-phone users in order to deliver ads tailored for that individual.

In advertising not to be different is virtually suicidal.

—William Bernbach, advertising legend and cofounder of the Doyle Dane Bernbach agency

When business is good it pays to advertise; when it is bad you have got to advertise.

—Red Auerbach, legendary coach of the Boston Celtics

The real axis of evil in America is the genius of our marketing and the gullibility of our people.

—Bill Maher, comedian and television host (from
When You Ride Alone You Ride with bin Laden, 2002)

The essence of trust building is to emphasize the similarities between you and the customer.

—Thomas J. Watson, chairman and CEO of IBM

—◆—

Don't blame the marketing department. The buck stops with the chief executive.

—John D. Rockefeller, industrialist, cofounder of Standard Oil Co., and philanthropist (from *John D. Rockefeller on Making Money: Advice and Words of Wisdom on Building*, 2015)

—◆—

The joy of music should never be interrupted by a commercial.

—Leonard Bernstein, composer/conductor

Advertising works most effectively when it's in line with what people are already trying to do.

—Mark Zuckerberg, cofounder and CEO of Facebook
(from *Time* magazine, July 17, 2007)

It is true that you may fool all of the people some of the time; you can even fool some of the people all the time; but you can't fool all of the people all the time.

—Abraham Lincoln, US president

It's just called "The Bible" now—we dropped the word "Holy" to give it a more mass-market appeal.

—Hodder & Stoughton, publisher/editor (from
The Daily Telegraph, December 30, 1989)

Transforming a brand into a socially responsible leader doesn't happen overnight by simply writing new marketing and advertising strategies. It takes effort to identify a vision that your customers will find credible and aligned with their values.

—Simon Mainwaring, advertising creative director and social media specialist (from website Mashable, April 22, 2011)

Advertisers in general bear a large part of the responsibility for the deep feelings of inadequacy that drive women to psychiatrists, pills, or the bottle.

—Marya Mannes, author and critic (from *But Will It Sell?*, 1964)

People don't believe what you tell them. They rarely believe what you show them. They often believe what their friends tell them. They always believe what they tell themselves.

—Seth Godin, author, entrepreneur, and public speaker

In day-to-day commerce, television is not so much interested in the business of communications as in the business of delivering audiences to advertisers. People are the merchandise, not the shows. The shows are merely the bait.

—Les Brown, songwriter, orchestra leader, and author (from *Television: The Business Behind the Box,* 1971)

I have . . . had a disturbing dream in which I break through a cave wall near Nag Hammadi and discover urns full of ancient Coptic scrolls. As I unfurl the first scroll, a subscription card to some Gnostic exercise magazine flutters out.

—Colin McEnroe, columnist and radio host

Advertising is the greatest art form of the 20th century.

—Marshall McLuhan, Canadian philosopher, futurist, and communications theorist (from *Advertising Age,* September 3, 1976)

Doing business without advertising is like winking at a girl in the dark. You know what you are doing but nobody else does.

> —Steuart Henderson Britt, marketing consultant, psychologist, and author (quoted in the *New York Herald Tribune*, October 30, 1956)

———❖———

Ensure your employees understand what your brand stands for so they can be your first line of word-of-mouth advertising.

> —Simon Mainwaring, advertising creative director and social media specialist (from website Mashable, April 22, 2011)

———❖———

When a man throws an empty cigarette package from an automobile, he is liable to a fine of $50. When a man throws a billboard across a view, he is richly rewarded.

> —Pat Brown (quoted in *Ogilvy on Advertising*, 1983)

The business that considers itself immune to the necessity for advertising sooner or later finds itself immune to business.

—Derby Brown

It is not unprofessional to give free legal advice, but advertising that the first visit will be free is a bit like a fox telling chickens he will not bite them until they cross the threshold of the hen house.

—Warren E. Burger, Chief Justice, US Supreme Court
(from State of the Judiciary speech to the American
Bar Association, 1986)

Advertising is the ability to sense, interpret . . . to put the very heart throbs of a business into type, paper and ink.

—Leo Burnett, founder of Leo Burnett Worldwide ad
agency

Chess is as elaborate a waste of human intelligence as you can find outside an advertising agency.

—Raymond Chandler, novelist and screenwriter (from the novel *The Long Goodbye*, 1953)

A tremendous amount of the entrepreneurial initiative, if you want to call it that, comes from the dynamic state sector on which most of the economy relies to socialize costs and risks and privatize eventual profit. And that's achieved by, if you like, advertising.

—Noam Chomsky, linguist, philosopher, cognitive scientist, historian, social critic, and political activist (from interview with *Democracy Now!*, April 3, 2006)

Advertising produces familiarity which produces sales.

—Paul Cookson, poet-performer

Advertising is the life of trade.

—Calvin Coolidge, US president (from *The International Dictionary of Thoughts,* 1969, compiled by John P. Bradley, Leo F. Daniels, and Thomas C. Jones)

We do not invest in advertising. . . . So racing is the best advertising for Ferrari.

—Luca Cordero di Montezemolo, former chairman of Fiat (from the *Wall Street Journal,* September 25, 2013)

You can tell the ideals of a nation by its advertisements.

—Norman Douglas, British writer (by fictional character Don Francesco in the novel *South Wind,* 1917)

Suppliers and especially manufacturers have market power because they have information about a product or a service that the customer does not and cannot have, and does not need if he can trust the brand. This explains the profitability of brands.

—Peter F. Drucker, management consultant, educator, and author (from *A Functioning Society: Community, Society, and Polity in the Twentieth Century,* 2011 edition)

Advertising isn't about truth or fairness or rationality, but about mobilising deeper and more primitive layers of the human mind.

—Brian Eno, musician, composer, and producer (from *The Guardian,* July 8, 2009)

Ads are the cave art of the twentieth century.

—Marshall McLuhan, Canadian philosopher, futurist, and communications theorist

The philosophy behind much advertising is based on the old observation that every man is really two men—the man he is and the man he wants to be.

—William Feather, publisher and author (quoted in
The Crown Treasury of Relevant Quotations, 1978)

Advertising isn't just the disruption of aesthetics, the insults to your intelligence and the interruption of your train of thought. At every company that sells ads, a significant portion of their engineering team spends their day tuning data mining, writing better code to collect all your personal data.

—Jan Koum, Internet entrepreneur and computer programmer (from *WhatsApp* blog, June 18, 2012)

The trouble with us in America isn't that the poetry of life has turned to prose, but that it has turned to advertising copy.

—Louis Kronenberger, critic and author (from "The Spirit of the Age," in *Company Manners*, 1954)

Mass demand has been created almost entirely through the development of advertising.

> —Calvin Coolidge, US president (from his address before the American Association of Advertising Agencies, October 27, 1926)

Society drives people crazy with lust and calls it advertising.

> —John Lahr, senior drama critic at *The New Yorker* magazine (from the *The Guardian*, August 2, 1989)

I view advertising as being this romanticizing element that helps us appreciate, understand and enjoy how remarkable it is that we've been able to do so much, and learn so much. I view it as really vital, even though sometimes it can be really annoying.

> —Jaron Lanier, computer scientist, author, and composer (from interview with technology publication *saydaily.com*, September 9, 2011)

Advertising may be described as the science of arresting the human intelligence long enough to get money from it.

—Stephen Butler Leacock, Canadian teacher, political scientist, writer, and humorist

———◆———

So long as there's a jingle in your head, television isn't free.

—Jason Love, marketing executive

———◆———

The secret of all effective originality in advertising is not the creation of new and tricky words and pictures, but one of putting familiar words and pictures into new relationships.

—Leo Burnett, founder of Leo Burnett Worldwide ad agency (from *100 Leo's: Wit & Wisdom from Leo Burnett*, 1995)

Nothing except the mint can make money without advertising.

—Thomas Babington Macaulay, British historian and Whig politician

❖

There is a great deal of advertising that is much better than the product. When that happens, all that the good advertising will do is put you out of business faster.

—Jerry Della Femina, advertising executive and restaurateur (from his book, *From Those Wonderful Folks Who Gave You Pearl Harbor: Front Line Dispatches from the Advertising War,* 1970)

❖

Our society's values are being corrupted by advertising's insistence on the equation: Youth equals popularity, popularity equals success, success equals happiness.

—John Fisher, British admiral (from his book *The Plot to Make You Buy,* 1968)

Advertising is a racket, like the movies and the brokerage business. You cannot be honest without admitting that its constructive contribution to humanity is exactly minus zero.

—F. Scott Fitzgerald, novelist (from a letter to his daughter published in *The Letters of F. Scott Fitzgerald,* 1963)

We grew up founding our dreams on the infinite promise of American advertising. I still believe that one can learn to play the piano by mail and that mud will give you a perfect complexion.

—Zelda Fitzgerald, socialite, novelist, and wife of F. Scott Fitzgerald (from her novel *Save Me the Waltz,* 1932)

Advertising is, of course, important because advertising is the final design. It's the last layer that speaks to the customer, that tells them what you have.

—Tom Ford, fashion designer (from interview with website The Daily Beast, December 12, 2009)

The essence of good advertising is not to inspire hope, but to create greed.

—Charles Adams, advertising executive

———◆———

Advertising—a judicious mixture of flattery and threats.

—Northrop Frye, Canadian literary critic (from *The Fitzhenry & Whiteside Book of Quotations*, 1993)

———◆———

Advertisements are now so numerous that they are very negligently perused, and it is therefore become necessary to gain attention by magnificence of promises and by eloquence sometimes sublime and sometimes pathetic.

—Samuel Johnson, British author (from his magazine *The Idler*, January 20, 1759)

Advertising is the lubricant for the free-enterprise system.

—Leo-Arthur Kelmenson, ad executive (from the *New York Times*, 1976)

———◆———

I love advertising, because I love self-promotion. I love mirror time, which is Me Time.

—Jarod Kintz, author

———◆———

Any time an investment company has to spend heavily on advertising, it's probably a bad business in which to invest.

—Robert Kiyosaki, author (from article on his website richdad.com, February 18, 2009)

When air conditioning, escalators, and advertising appeared, shopping expanded its scale, but also limited its spontaneity. And it became much more predictable, almost scientific. What had once been the most surprising became the most manipulated.

> —Rem Koolhaas, Dutch architect, architectural theorist, urbanist, and Harvard professor (from interview with indexmagazine.com, 2000)

———◆———

Ideally, advertising aims at the goal of a programmed harmony among all human impulses and aspirations and endeavors. Using handicraft methods, it stretches out toward the ultimate electronic goal of a collective consciousness.

> —Marshall McLuhan, Canadian philosopher, futurist, and communications theorist (from his book *Understanding Media: The Extensions of Man*, 1964)

———◆———

I am one who believes that one of the greatest dangers of advertising is not that of misleading people, but that of boring them to death.

> —Leo Burnett, founder of Leo Burnett Worldwide ad agency

History will see advertising as one of the real evil things of our time. It is stimulating people constantly to want things, want this, want that.

> —Malcolm Muggeridge, journalist and broadcaster (quoted in the book *The Want Makers: Inside the World of Advertising*, 1988)

———

I think that I shall never see/A billboard lovely as a tree/Perhaps, unless the billboards fall/I'll never see a tree at all.

> —Ogden Nash, poet (from his poem "Song of the Open Road," published in *The New Yorker*, October 15, 1932)

———

I know that campaigns can seem small, and even silly. Trivial things become big distractions. Serious issues become sound bites. And the truth gets buried under an avalanche of money and advertising. If you're sick of hearing me approve this message, believe me—so am I.

> —Barack Obama, US president (speaking at the Democratic National Convention, 2012)

Advertising in the final analysis should be news. If it is not news it is worthless.

—Adolph S. Ochs, newspaper publisher (from article in the *Indiana Gazette*, March 26, 1958)

It takes a big idea to attract the attention of consumers and get them to buy your product. Unless your advertising contains a big idea, it will pass like a ship in the night. I doubt if more than one campaign in a hundred contains a big idea.

—David Ogilvy, founder of Ogilvy & Mather ad agency (quoted in *Ogilvy on Advertising*, 1983)

Promise, large promise, is the soul of an advertisement.

—Samuel Johnson, British author (from his magazine *The Idler*, January 20, 1759)

Anyone who thinks that people can be fooled or pushed around has an inaccurate and pretty low estimate of people—and he won't do very well in advertising.

> —Leo Burnett, founder of Leo Burnett Worldwide ad agency

The business of the advertiser is to see that we go about our business with some magic spell or tune or slogan throbbing quietly in the background of our minds.

> —Marshall McLuhan, Canadian philosopher, futurist, and communications theorist (from his book *Understanding Media: The Extensions of Man,* 1964)

Advertising is the rattling of a stick inside a swill bucket.

> —George Orwell, novelist, essayist, journalist, and critic (from his novel *Keep the Aspidistra Flying,* 1936)

Vertical search engines that match your business, service or products with a target market offer you a higher conversion rate than traditional search engines. Because they have already qualified their interest by coming to a search engine with a specific focus, searchers will be more receptive to targeted advertising.

—Marc Ostrofsky, Internet entrepreneur and author
(from huffingtonpost.com, January 12, 2012)

The word "you" is the most important word in the English language, as far as writing advertising copy is concerned. People respond to this word because they like talking about themselves and being talked about in a positive manner.

—Peter J. Patsula, founder of Patsula Media and author
(from his online publication *The Entrepreneur's Guidebook Series*, 2001–2007)

Living in an age of advertisement, we are perpetually disillusioned.

—J. B. Priestley, English playwright, novelist, biographer, literary critic, screenwriter, and broadcaster (from his book *The Balconinny and Other Essays*, 1929)

When the historian of the Twentieth Century shall have finished his narrative, and comes searching for the subtitle which shall best express the spirit of the period, we think it not at all unlikely that he may select "The Age of Advertising" for the purpose.

—*Printers' Ink* monthly, May 27, 1915

Advertising, music, atmospheres, subliminal messages and films can have an impact on our emotional life, and we cannot control it because we are not even conscious of it.

—Tariq Ramadan, Swiss academic, philosopher and writer (from his book *The Quest for Meaning: Developing a Philosophy of Pluralism,* 2010)

Never stop testing, and your advertising will never stop improving.

—David Ogilvy, founder of Ogilvy & Mather ad agency (from his book *Confessions of an Advertising Man,* 1963)

24

Creative without strategy is called "art." Creative with strategy is called "advertising."

> —Jef I. Richards, professor of advertising

———◆◆◆———

Advertising is the art of convincing people to spend money they don't have for something they don't need.

> —Will Rogers, American cowboy, vaudeville performer, humorist, newspaper columnist, social commentator, and stage and motion picture actor

———◆◆◆———

The work of an advertising agency is warmly and immediately human. It deals with human needs, wants, dreams and hopes. Its "product" cannot be turned out on an assembly line.

> —Leo Burnett, founder of Leo Burnett Worldwide ad agency

There are huge advertising budgets only when there's no difference between the products. If the products really were different, people would buy the one that's better. Advertising teaches people not to trust their judgment. Advertising teaches people to be stupid.

>—Carl Sagan, astronomer, cosmologist, astrophysicist, and author (from his book *Contact*, 1985)

Advertising is the modern substitute for argument; its function is to make the worse appear the better.

>—George Santayana, philosopher, essayist, poet, and novelist

---

Google was founded to get information to everybody. A by-product of that strategy is that we invented an advertising business which has provided great economics that allows us to build the servers, hire the employees, create value.

>—Eric Schmidt, executive chairman of Alphabet Inc., formerly Google (from article in *The Guardian*, April 19, 2013)

Don't bore your reader. You can't bore people into buying your products or services. If your ad is boring then it probably means your company and your products are also boring.

> —Peter J. Patsula, founder of Patsula Media and author (from his online publication *The Entrepreneur's Guidebook Series*, 2001–2007)

Advertising is an environmental striptease for a world of abundance.

> —Marshal McLuhan, Canadian philosopher, futurist, and communications theorist (quoted in *Subliminal Seduction: Ad Media's Manipulation of a Not So Innocent America*, 1974)

Don't Tell My Mother I Work in an Advertising Agency— She Thinks I Play Piano in a Whorehouse.

> —Jacques Seguela, cofounder of French advertising agency RSCG (title of his 1979 autobiography)

A lot of advertising has gotten worse. I think it's kind of lost its nerve, to be honest with you. I feel like the advertising of the '60s, they were nervier. You know why? Because there was less at stake.

—Jerry Seinfeld, comedian, actor, writer, and producer (interview with *Adweek*, December 17, 2013)

Advertising is the art of making whole lies out of half truths.

—Edgar A. Shoaff, entrepreneur and motivational speaker

Starbucks is not an advertiser; people think we are a great marketing company, but in fact we spend very little money on marketing and more money on training our people than advertising.

—Howard Schultz, CEO of Starbucks (from interview with CNN.com, December 28, 2007)

What is the difference between unethical and ethical advertising? Unethical advertising uses falsehoods to deceive the public; ethical advertising uses truth to deceive the public.

 —Vilhjalmur Stefansson, Canadian explorer and ethnologist (from his autobiography *Discovery*, 1964)

———◆◆◆———

With no ads, who would pay for the media? The good fairy?

 —Samuel Thurm, senior vice president, US Association of National Advertisers

———◆◆◆———

Early to bed, early to rise, work like hell, and advertise.

 —Ted Turner, founder of Turner Broadcasting and CNN (from Montana State University–Northern commencement address, May 2011)

Good advertising does not just circulate information. It penetrates the public mind with desires and belief.

> —Leo Burnett, founder of Leo Burnett Worldwide ad agency (from *100 Leo's: Wit & Wisdom from Leo Burnett*, 1995)

Many a small thing has been made large by the right kind of advertising.

> —Mark Twain, humorist and writer (from his novel *A Connecticut Yankee in King Arthur's Court*, 1889)

Advertisers constantly invent cures to which there is no disease.

> —Unknown

Any seeming deception in a statement is costly, not only in the expense of the advertising but in the detrimental effect produced upon the customer, who believes she has been misled.

> —John Wanamaker, department-store magnate (from *Whatever Happened to Madison Avenue?*, 1991)

Advertising is legalized lying.

> —H. G. Wells, writer (from *Crown's Book of Political Quotations*, 1982)

We have always said that advertising is just the icing on the cake. It is not the cake.

> —Meg Whitman, chairman and CEO of Hewlett-Packard

As advertising blather becomes the nation's normal idiom, language becomes printed noise.

—George Will, newspaper columnist and political commentator

——◆——

We are a consumer company and our success is directly linked to our users trusting us. Therefore, we have the same incentive as the user: they want to see relevant advertising so their experience of Google is positive and we want to deliver it.

—Susan Wojcicki, CEO of YouTube (from interview in *The Telegraph,* December 4, 2010)

——◆——

Half the money I spend on advertising is wasted; the trouble is, I don't know which half.

—John Wanamaker, department-store magnate (quoted in David Ogilvy's *Confessions of an Advertising Man,* 1963)

Advertising says to people, "Here's what we've got. Here's what it will do for you. Here's how to get it."

> —Leo Burnett, founder of Leo Burnett Worldwide ad agency (from *100 Leo's: Wit & Wisdom from Leo Burnett,* 1995)

Business

The world has 7.5 billion people, and most have had an observation about business, a universal pursuit as old as mankind and unavoidable in modern life. Most of the 7.5 billion viewpoints are valid. As merchant, consumer, or vendor, each person occupies the business ecosystem, however primitive or advanced. What follow are resonant musings on the topic by notables the world over.

A larger business is not merely a bigger small business; it is a related but new entity.

—Nick Lyons, teacher, writer, and publisher

Care for your infant business or career as you would care for your infant child—with loving attention, with no expectation of any reward, being in the moment with it, accepting it as is, watching it grow, enjoying every step of the way.

—Marc Allen, publisher and author (from his book *The Millionaire Course: A Visionary Plan for Creating the Life of Your Dreams*, 2003)

It takes more than capital to swing business. You've got to have the A.I.D. degree to get by— Advertising, Initiative, and Dynamics.

—Isaac Asimov, author and professor of biochemistry

That's one thing we never did much of while we were building Wal-Mart, talk about ourselves or do a whole lot of bragging outside the Wal-Mart family—except when we had to convince some banker or some Wall Street financier that we intended to amount to something someday, that we were worth taking a chance on.

—Sam Walton, founder of Wal-Mart

Online business models are still evolving. New and different products and services pop up every day. This gives rise to supporting products and services. A business can make substantial profit by helping others execute their plans for making money.

—Marc Ostrofsky, author, entrepreneur, and investor (from his book *Get Rich Click: The Ultimate Guide to Making Money on the Internet,* 2011)

I should say in general the advantage of education is to better fit a man for life's work. I would advise young men to take a college course, as a rule, but think some are just as well off with a thorough business training.

—John D. Rockefeller, industrialist, cofounder of Standard Oil Co., and philanthropist

Going after a target market larger than your ability to serve can lead to bankruptcy, not fortune—greed is no substitute for good planning. On the other hand, going after a target market too small to support your business is just plain silly. A target market must be big enough to earn a profit.

—Peter J. Patsula, author and founder of Patsula Media (from his online publication *The Entrepreneur's Guidebook Series,* 2001–2007)

———

Business is a combination of war and sport.

—Andre Maurois, French author (from *National Catholic Reporter,* October 27, 1991)

———

I tell young entrepreneurs to use the leader in their industry and as a benchmark as they work to create their own brand. Don't look at what your competition is doing—if you emulate the leader in your industry, you will achieve a higher level of engagement with consumers and make their buying experience richer.

—Steve Stoute, advertising executive and marketing expert (from CNN.Money.com, October 3, 2011)

In general, an asset should be sold when it has greater value to a buyer. This happens when a buyer has a complimentary business or capability that would enable them to do more with that business. Many businesses we have exited were not failures, but had simply reached a point in their life cycle where they no longer provided a core capability or served as a platform for growth.

—Charles Koch, co-owner of Koch Industries

In industries where a lot of competitors are selling the same product—mangoes, gasoline, DVD players—price is the easiest way to distinguish yourself. The hope is that if you cut prices enough you can increase your market share, and even your profits. But this works only if your competitors won't, or can't, follow suit.

—James Surowiecki, journalist (from *The New Yorker* magazine, November 9, 2009)

If the spirit of business adventure is dulled, this country will cease to hold the foremost position in the world.

—Andrew Mellon, banker, industrialist, philanthropist, and US ambassador

The Internet is the Viagra of big business.

—Jack Welch, GE chairman and CEO (addressing the
sixth annual World Business Forum, October 2010)

❦

Business after all is a form of warfare; you bring all your
available weapons to bear. If you don't you're a fool.

—Cornell Woolrich, novelist (from his novella *Jane
Brown's Body,* 1938)

❦

The essence of a successful business is really quite simple.
It is your ability to offer a product or service that people
will pay for at a price sufficiently above your costs, ideally three or four or five times your cost, thereby giving
you a profit that enables you to buy and to offer more
products and services.

—Brian Tracy, author (from Entrepreneur.com, July 7,
2004)

If you can build a business up big enough, it's respectable.

—Will Rogers, American cowboy, vaudeville performer, humorist, newspaper columnist, social commentator, and stage and motion picture actor

Business is not financial science, it's about trading . . . buying and selling. It's about creating a product or service so good that people will pay for it.

—Anita Roddick, founder of the Body Shop (from AnitaRoddick.com)

Every great business is built on friendship.

—J. C. Penney, founder of retail chain JCPenney

Corporations are like protean bacteria; you hit them with accountability and they mutate and change their names.

—Doug Anderson, author

The primary advantage of [a partnership] business formation is the pooling of talent, experience, and capital. However, dual or multiple ownership structures can lead to serious complications if the relationships between individuals break down. Quite often, the *pool* becomes a *drain*.

—Peter J. Patsula, founder of Patsula Media and author

People are definitely a company's greatest asset. It doesn't make any difference whether the product is cars or cosmetics. A company is only as good as the people it keeps.

—Mary Kay Ash, founder of Mary Kay Cosmetics

Corporations are social organizations, the theater in which men and women realize or fail to realize purposeful and productive lives.

—Lester Bangs, music journalist, critic, author, and musician

———————

Corporation, n., An ingenious device for obtaining profit without individual responsibility.

—Ambrose Bierce, journalist and author (from his book *The Devil's Dictionary*, 1911)

———————

If only one didn't know that at the secret heart of all such organizations, corporations and governments alike, it still came down to a finite number of fallible people talking to each other. . . .

—Lois McMaster Bujold, author (from her book *Cryoburn,* 2010)

In large organizations the dilution of information as it passes up and down the hierarchy, and horizontally across departments, can undermine the effort to focus on common goals.

—Mihaly Csikszentmihalyi, psychologist and author (from his book *Good Business: Leadership, Flow, and the Making of Meaning,* 2003)

The fact that the United States has political, economic, and legal structures that do indeed create incentives to control hazards (in the workplace) is one of the reasons the corporations have moved to Latin America and Asia.

—Vincent A. Gallagher, author and safety expert (from his book *The True Cost of Low Prices: The Violence of Globalization,* 2006)

A corporation is a living organism; it has to continue to shed its skin. Methods have to change. Focus has to change. Values have to change. The sum total of those changes is transformation.

—Andrew Grove, chairman of Intel (from interview with *Esquire* magazine, January 29, 2007)

It's not a question of arriving and putting in a whole new administration, but instead, arriving and "compacting" things as much as possible, reducing management layers. We want as few management layers as possible, so that executives are very close to the operations. We also don't believe in having big corporate infrastructures.

—Carlos Slim Helu, billionaire Mexican industrialist (from *BusinessWeek* magazine, February 21, 2000)

Any corporate policy and plan which is typical of the industry is doomed to mediocrity.

—Bruce Henderson, founder of the Boston Consulting Group

We have bloated bureaucracies in Corporate America. The root of the problem is the absence of real corporate democracy.

—Carl Icahn, investor

The most important thing I've learned since becoming CEO is context. It's how your company fits in with the world and how you respond to it.

> —Jeffrey Immelt, chairman and CEO of GE (from interview with *Fast Company* magazine, April 1, 2004)

⬥

The trouble, in my opinion, with corporate America today, is that everything is thought of in quarters.

> —Henry Kravis, investor and financier (from interview with American Academy of Achievement)

⬥

So often corporate America, business America, are the worst communicators, because all they understand are facts, and they cannot tell a story. They know how to explain their quarterly results, but they don't know how to explain what they mean.

> —Frank Luntz, political consultant and pollster (from PBS's *Frontline* show, November 9, 2004)

Give tax breaks to large corporations, so that money can trickle down to the general public, in the form of extra jobs.

—Andrew Mellon, banker, industrialist, and philanthropist

———◆———

A business absolutely devoted to service will have only one worry about profits. They will be embarrassingly large.

—Henry Ford, founder of Ford Motor Co. (Ford Motors PR compilation)

———◆———

In business, you don't get what you deserve, you get what you negotiate.

—Chester L. Karrass, negotiations expert and author

One of the most-common misconceptions about our private enterprise system is that large companies, such as the Fortune 500, are integral to the process of job creation in this country. The truth is quite the opposite.

>—Michael Milken, former financier
> (from mikemilken.com)

The great corporations of this country were not founded by ordinary people. They were founded by people with extraordinary intelligence, ambition, and aggressiveness.

>—Daniel Patrick Moynihan, politician and sociologist

A friendship founded on business is better than a business founded on friendship.

>—John D. Rockefeller, industrialist, cofounder of Standard Oil Co., and philanthropist

There are bad people and there are bad corporations. Just as there are good people and good corporations. That might seem too black and white, but what can I tell ya?

—James Murdoch, CEO of 21st Century Fox (from interview in *The Guardian*, June 6, 2009)

———

Great corporations exist only because they are created and safeguarded by our institutions; and it is therefore our right and duty to see that they work in harmony with these institutions.

—Theodore Roosevelt, US president (from his *Message Communicated to the Two Houses of Congress at the Beginning of the First Session of the Fifty-Seventh Congress*, December 3, 1901)

———

We also need to reduce corporate tax rates. This applies to small, medium and large businesses. At 35 percent, we have the second highest corporate rates in the world. It restricts the growth of small enterprises that need to plow capital back into their businesses and forces companies and jobs to move overseas.

—Meg Whitman, CEO of Hewlett Packard Enterprise

Business is always interfering with pleasure—but it makes other pleasures possible.

—William Feather, publisher and author

❖

All business is basically about customers and marketing and making money and capitalism and winning and promoting it and having something someone really wants. If you look at the Dairy Queen model it pretty much works for almost everything. You know what you're doing and you know who your customers are and if you don't drop too much ice cream, chances are you can make a living.

—Roger Ailes, former chairman of Fox News Channel and Fox Television (*Financial Times,* October 6, 2006)

❖

Business is all about solving people's problems—at a profit.

—Paul Marsden, writer and businessman

Big thinking precedes great achievement.

—Wilferd Peterson, author

⊰•⊱

Few people do business well who do nothing else.

—Lord Chesterfield, British statesman, diplomat, and wit (from a letter to his son in *The Works of Lord Chesterfield: Including His Letters to His Son, Etc: to which is Prefixed, an Original Life of the Author,* 1855)

⊰•⊱

Business is the salt of life.

—Thomas Fuller, English physician, writer, and adage collector

A business may have to reinvent itself every day but it must never forget the guidelines that enabled it to grow and flourish in the first place.

—Nick Lyons, teacher, writer, and publisher

———◆◆◆———

A market is never saturated with a good product, but it is very quickly saturated with a bad one.

—Henry Ford, founder of Ford Motor Co.

———◆◆◆———

Relationships are the only thing that matter in business in life.

—Jerry Weintraub, movie producer (from his book *When I Stop Talking, You'll Know I'm Dead: Useful Stories from a Persuasive Man,* 2010)

I always like to refer to managers in corporate America as the renters of the corporate assets, not the owners.

> —Henry Kravis, investor and financier (from interview with American Academy of Achievement)

—◆—

Networking is like fishing. Just give some beer and a boat and I'll be in business.

> —Jarod Kintz, author (from his *This Book Is Not for Sale*, 2011)

—◆—

Most men have professions, yet few act like professionals.

> —Chris Murray, author, inspirational speaker, and business coach (from his book *The Extremely Successful Salesman's Club*, 2014)

Work expands so as to fill the time available for its completion.

> —Cyril Northcote Parkinson, British naval historian
> and author (from his essay in *The Economist* in 1955)

A business like an automobile, has to be driven, in order to get results.

> —B. C. Forbes, founder of *Forbes Magazine*

The minute you stop caring about your business is the same minute your business stops caring about you.

> —Steven Ivy, attorney and entrepreneur

If we only have great companies, we will merely have a prosperous society, not a great one. Economic growth and power are the means, not the definition, of a great nation.

—Jim Collins, business consultant, author, and lecturer

Live together like brothers and do business like strangers.

—Arabian proverb

The more businesses you have, the less work you do.

—Ehab Atalla, author (from his book *The Secrets of Business,* 2013)

Everything can be improved.
—C. W. Barron, owner of Dow Jones Co. and founder
of *Barron's* magazine

Under promise and over deliver.
—Toby Bloomberg, strategy and social media
consultant

A business has to be involving, it has to be fun, and it
has to exercise your creative instincts.
—Sir Richard Branson, billionaire entrepreneur and
founder of Virgin Airlines

In business or in life, don't follow the wagon tracks too closely.

> —H. Jackson Brown Jr., author (from his *The Complete Life's Little Instruction Book*, 1991)

***

The most important thing is to enjoy yourself and continue to work. I know life is a journey, not a destination. That's also true in business. Your objectives keep moving.

> —Thomas J. Burrell, founder of Burrell Communications

***

Give the public everything you can give them, keep the place as clean as you can keep it, keep it friendly.

> —Walt Disney, founder of Walt Disney Studios and theme parks

Company cultures are like country cultures. Never try to change one. Try, instead, to work with what you've got.

> —Peter F. Drucker, management consultant, educator, and author

In business, three things are necessary: knowledge, temper, and time.

> —Owen Felltham, English writer (from his book *Resolves, Divine, Moral, Political, of Owen Felltham,* 1620)

Drive thy business, let not that drive thee.

> —Benjamin Franklin, US founding father and inventor

In business, the idea of measuring what you are doing, picking the measurements that count like customer satisfaction and performance . . . you thrive on that.

—Bill Gates, cofounder of Microsoft and philanthropist (from Politico.com, March 13, 2013)

———◆◆◆———

Every business has competition. Even the American Football League has to compete with basketball, hockey and other forms of entertainment. Every business also wants to beat the competition, steal its market share or perhaps even drive it into bankruptcy. But when starting out, realize that competition isn't necessarily a bad thing. It shows there's already some demand for the goods or services you intend to offer. In fact, no competition is usually something that should be treated with caution not jubilation.

—Peter J. Patsula, founder of Patsula Media and author (from his online publication *The Entrepreneur's Guidebook Series,* 2001–2007, Guidebook #47, "Spying on the Competition")

There is at least one point in the history of any company when you have to change dramatically to rise to the next level of performance. Miss that moment—and you start to decline.

—Andy Grove, chairman and CEO of Intel (from *Fortune* magazine, February 22, 1993)

———◆◆———

You have to have your heart in the business and the business in your heart.

—Thomas Jefferson, founding father and president

———◆◆———

Life is not high school—there is no penalty for copying the smart kid's homework. The trick is to figure out who that kid is and how to hire him or her.

—Mike Jones, CEO of Science Inc. (from Entrepreneur.com, January 6, 2014)

The business of America is business.

—Calvin Coolidge, US president

———

I think it's very important that whatever you're trying to make or sell, or teach has to be basically good. A bad product and you know what? You won't be here in ten years.

—Martha Stewart, businesswoman

———

Why are we here? I think many people assume, wrongly, that a company exists solely to make money. Money is an important part of a company's existence, if the company is any good. But a result is not a cause. We have to go deeper and find the real reason for our being.

—David Packard, cofounder of Hewlett-Packard

It is critical to learn how to listen for what is not being said.

—Debra Kaye, composer

—⊰◆⊱—

Business is never so healthy as when, like a chicken, it must do a certain amount of scratching for what it gets.

—Henry Ford, founder of Ford Motor Co.

—⊰◆⊱—

Whenever you're sitting across from some important person, always picture him sitting there in a suit of long red underwear. That's the way I always operated in business.

—Joseph P. Kennedy, businessman, diplomat, and patriarch of the Kennedy political clan

Your first 20 hires will make or break your company. Look for top-notch intrinsic qualities, and refuse to compromise.

—Vinod Khosla, cofounder of Sun Microsystems (from LinkedIn advice column, February 25, 2014)

———◆———

Three rules of good negotiation: 1. Know what the other party wants. 2. Listen carefully. 3. Don't let your emotions get in the way of a good deal.

—Betty Liu, Bloomberg TV anchor (from her book *Work Smarts*, 2014)

———◆———

You must not offend a man, and then send him to fill an important office or command.

—Machiavelli, Italian Renaissance political philosopher

Life is too short to be a boring company.

> —Andrew Mason, founder and CEO of Groupon Inc.
> (from Groupon's initial public offering document,
> June 2, 2011)

———◆———

Talk of nothing but business, and dispatch that business
quickly.

> —Andre Maurois, French author

———◆———

The first principle of contract negotiation is don't remind
them of what you did in the past; tell them what you're
going to do in the future.

> —Stan Musial, storied Hall of Fame player with the St.
> Louis Cardinals

If you're trying to create a company, it's like baking a cake. You have to have all the ingredients in the right proportion.

—Elon Musk, founder of Tesla Motors and SpaceX (from *Los Angeles Times* interview, August 1, 2012)

Think globally, act locally. When negotiating, think communally, act personally.

—Sheryl Sandberg, chief operating officer of Facebook (from her book *Lean In: Women, Work, and the Will to Lead,* 2013)

As a small businessperson, you have no greater leverage than the truth.

—John Greenleaf Whittier, American Quaker poet and slavery abolitionist

You're either making money or you're not. If you're not making money get out of the business.

—Meredith Whitney, financial analyst

———

Going to work for a large company is like getting on a train. Are you going sixty miles an hour or is the train going sixty miles an hour and you're just sitting still?

—J. Paul Getty, founder of Getty Oil Company

———

Without some dissimulation no business can be carried on at all.

—Alexander Pope, English poet

A truly well-built business has taken too much time, love, vision, energy, effort, thought, problem-solving, blood to risk on one—or even a dozen—rolls of the dice. Anyway, it's infinitely more fun, and infinitely more satisfying to grow a business steadily—against any odds.

—Nick Lyons, teacher, writer, and publisher

—◆◆—

You can't tax business. Business doesn't pay taxes. It collects taxes.

—Ronald Reagan, US President

—◆◆—

Profit is an illusion, cash flow is fact.

—Unknown

What helps people, helps business.

—Leo Burnett, founder of Leo Burnett Worldwide ad
agency

———◆———

A small profit is better than a big loss.

—Ron Rash, poet, short story writer, and novelist

———◆———

Mention the word accounting, and otherwise competent business men and women suddenly grit their teeth,
furrow their foreheads, and start uncontrollably pulling
out chunks of their own hair. Why is this? How can a
craft, which is nothing more than a tool to keep track
of the inflow and outflow of cash, be thought of with
such contempt and fear? The mystery becomes even
more puzzling once you realize that ACCOUNTING is
essentially the discipline of counting money. And since
most people start a business to make money, it seems
rather silly they shouldn't enjoy counting it.

—Peter J. Patsula, founder of Patsula Media and author
(from his online publication *The Entrepreneur's Guidebook Series,* 2001–2007)

Humor

With a gross domestic product valued at about $18 *trillion*, the US economy is serious business—too serious, in the sober judgments of two sources that periodically monitor the emotional pulse of the American workplace. According to the *Harvard Business Review*, on-the-job humorlessness is constraining productivity, creativity, and collaboration. And the humor drought exists even though 91 percent of executives believe that a sense of humor boosts careers, according to Robert Half International, a top human resource consulting firm. Yet it seems that the only time business leaders deign to release their inner comedian is in the opening lines of a speech before a somber business audience.

The levity deficit in American office buildings and factories seems puzzling, given the plethora of witty quotes below. They indicate that the funny bone is sharp within the labor force across occupational fields.

Business is like sex. When it's good, it's very, very good; when it's not so good, it's still good.

> —George Katona, business analyst (from the *Wall Street Journal*, April 9, 1969)

Big business never pays a nickel in taxes, according to Ralph Nader, who represents a big consumer organization that never pays a nickel in taxes.

> —Dave Barry, columnist

The purpose of bureaucracy is to compensate for incompetence and lack of discipline.

> —Jim Collins, business consultant, author, and lecturer (from his book *Good to Great: Why Some Companies Make the Leap . . . and Others Don't,* 2001)

But while my inner voice was clearly telling me I was at my core an entrepreneur, it's inconvenient to decide at twenty-three that you can't really work for other people.

—Kelly Cutrone, fashion publicist (from her book *If You Have to Cry, Go Outside: And Other Things Your Mother Never Told You*)

In business, sir, one has no friends, only correspondents.

—Alexandre Dumas, writer

Even if you're on the right track, you'll get run over if you just sit there.

—Will Rogers, American cowboy, vaudeville performer, humorist, newspaper columnist, social commentator, and stage and motion picture actor

Be the kind of person who catches the shit before it hits the fan, not the one who scrapes it off afterwards.

—Jonas Eriksson, writer (from his book *The Wake-Up Call*)

———◆———

Long-range planning works best in the short term.

—Doug Evelyn, Smithsonian Institution executive

———◆———

Quality means doing it right when no one is looking.

—Henry Ford, founder of Ford Motor Co.

There is one rule for industrialists and that is: make the best quality goods possible at the lowest cost possible, paying the highest wages possible.

—Henry Ford, founder of Ford Motor Co.

People are best convinced by things they themselves discover.

—Benjamin Franklin, US founding father and inventor

I have come to the conclusion that my subjective account of my motivation is largely mythical on almost all occasions. I don't know why I do things.

—J. B. S. Haldane, scientist

Behind every successful man is a proud wife and a surprised mother-in-law.

—Hubert H. Humphrey, US vice president

         —◆—

What does it mean to be the best? It means you have to be better than the number two guy. But what gratification is there in that? He's a loser—that's why he's number two.

—Jarod Kintz, writer (from his book *This Book Is Not for Sale*)

         —◆—

I'm Phil Knight, and I don't believe in advertising.

—Phil Knight, Nike founder (from *Vanity Fair* magazine, August 1993)

The greatest irony is that people with Rolodexes are no longer LinkedIn. And if that pun doesn't make sense, don't ask anyone in your Rolodex to explain it.

—Ryan Lilly, writer (from his book *#Networking is people looking for people looking for people*)

You don't have to reinvent the wheel . . . just steal the hubcaps.

—Michael P. Naughton, musician

There are two reasons why some people don't mind their own business. One is that they have no mind, and the other is that they have no business.

—Vikrant Parsai, author

A computer lets you make more mistakes faster than any invention in human history—with the possible exceptions of handguns and tequila.

—Mitch Ratliffe, writer (from *Technology Review* article, April 1992)

———◆———

People are not like a business. You can't buy and sell them like so much property. You can't lock them up in a vault and expect them to appreciate it.

—Harold Robbins, novelist (from his book *Never Leave Me*)

———◆———

A computer doesn't charge for overtime and doesn't get healthcare benefits.

—Adam Smith, TV business commentator

Beware of any enterprise requiring new clothes.

—Henry David Thoreau, author, poet, philosopher, abolitionist, and naturalist

———◆———

My son is now an "entrepreneur." That's what you're called when you don't have a job.

—Ted Turner, media mogul

———◆———

All you need in this life is ignorance and confidence; then success is sure.

—Mark Twain, author and humorist

A consultant is someone who takes the watch off your wrist and tells you the time.

—Unknown

Women will never be as successful as men because they have no wives to advise them.

—Dick Van Dyke, actor and comedian

My own business always bores me to death; I prefer other people's.

—Oscar Wilde, Irish playwright, novelist, essayist, and poet

A meeting is an event at which the minutes are kept and the hours are lost.

—Unknown

⬥

My dream was actually just to have a computer some day. If I'd imagined that it meant starting a company to sell them, I probably would have avoided the whole thing.

—Steve Wozniak, inventor and cofounder of Apple

⬥

I think it's wrong that only one company makes the game Monopoly.

—Steven Wright, comedian

The best way to engage honestly with the marketplace via Twitter is to never use the words "engage," "honestly," or "marketplace."

—Jeffrey Zeldman, web designer and entrepreneur

I'm not a businessman, I'm a business, man!

—Jay-Z, rapper and entertainment mogul

I have a business appointment that I am anxious . . . to miss.

—Oscar Wilde, Irish playwright, novelist, essayist, and poet

I work for a mom-and-pop business. They're my mom and pop, and by work I mean they give me an allowance.

—Jarod Kintz, writer (from his book *At even one penny, this book would be overpriced. In fact, free is too expensive, because you'd still waste time by reading it*)

All paid jobs absorb and degrade the mind.

—Aristotle, philosopher

Never put off until tomorrow what you can avoid altogether.

—Unknown

Rise early, work hard, strike oil.
—J. Paul Getty, founder of Getty Oil Co.

I owe my success to having listened respectfully to the very best advice, and then going away and doing the exact opposite.
—G. K. Chesterton, poet and philosopher

The early bird gets the worm, but the second mouse gets the cheese.
—Willie Nelson, musician

Nobody talks more of free enterprise and competition and of the best man winning than the man who inherited his father's store or farm.

　　—C. Wright Mills, sociologist

Any man of reasonable intelligence can make money if that's what he wants. Mostly it's women or clothes or admiration he really wants and they deflect him.

　　—John Steinbeck, author (from his novel *The Winter of Our Discontent*, 1961)

A banker: the person who lends you his umbrella when the sun is shining and wants it back the minute it rains.

　　—Anonymous

Crying about the economy is a strategy. It won't get you a job, but it will keep Kleenex in business.

—Jarod Kintz, writer (from his book *99 Cents for Some Nonsense,* 2012)

Millionaires are marrying their secretaries because they are so busy making money they haven't time to see other girls.

—Doris Lilly, gossip columnist

When I first starting making money, when I first made my first six digits, I was—my big thing was I went to put super unleaded in my truck for the first time.

—Matthew McConaughey, actor

You read a book from beginning to end. You run a business the opposite way. You start with the end, and then you do everything you must to reach it.
    —Harold S. Geneen, chairman of ITT Corp.

Business is the art of extracting money from another man's pocket without resorting to violence.
    —Bette Davis, actress

In the business world an executive knows something about everything, a technician knows everything about something, and the switchboard operator knows everything.
    —Harold Coffin, former humor columnist for the Associated Press

Customers

The customer is the engine of any economic system, the raison d'être of any business. As such, the customer is perhaps the most complex factor for business owners, economists, policymakers, and manufacturers—indeed, for all other participants in an economy—to thoroughly understand. What are customers' needs? What are their emotional states? How can they be reached most effectively with come-ons?

At the same time, the customer rules. Economists, for example, seek to gauge "consumer sentiment"—a person's attitude about her financial health, the state of the economy, and her outlook toward the economic future. "Consumer debt" is tracked persistently. So, too, are the costs of their purchases—the "consumer price index." Never forget, the customer is always king.

We demand that big business give people a square deal; in return we must insist that when anyone engaged in big business honestly endeavors to do right, he shall himself be given a square deal.

> —Theodore Roosevelt, US president (from his letter to Sir Edward Gray, November 15, 1913)

Customers today want the very most and the very best for the very least amount of money, and on the best terms. Only the individuals and companies that provide absolutely excellent products and services at absolutely excellent prices will survive.

> —Brian Tracy, author (from his book *Earn What You're Really Worth: Maximize Your Income at Any Time in Any Market*, 2010)

Your company's most valuable asset is how it is known to its customers.

> —Theodore Levitt, economist, professor at Harvard Business School, and author (from his book *The Marketing Imagination*, 1986)

There is only one boss. The customer. And he can fire everybody in the company from the chairman on down, simply by spending his money somewhere else.
—Sam Walton, founder of Wal-Mart

The essence of trust building is to emphasize the similarities between you and the customer.
—Thomas J. Watson, chairman and CEO of IBM

The first step in exceeding your customer's expectations is to know those expectations.
—Roy H. Williams, author and marketing consultant

Revolve your world around the customer and more customers will revolve around you.

—Heather Williams, author

———◆———

Many companies expect loyal customers without providing loyal service. This has been the visionary failure of countless corporations.

—Steve Maraboli, author and speaker

———◆———

Statistics suggest that when customers complain, business owners and managers ought to get excited about it. The complaining customer represents a huge opportunity for more business.

—Zig Ziglar, author and motivational speaker

The customer's perception is your reality.

—Kate Zabriskie, author (from her book *Customer Service Excellence: How to Deliver Value to Today's Busy Customer*, 2009)

———◆———

Know what your customers want most and what your company does best. Focus on where those two meet.

—Kevin Stirtz, author and web marketing consultant

———◆———

The most important adage and the only adage is, the customer comes first, whatever the business, the customer comes first.

—Kerry Stokes, Australian broadcast billionaire (from interview with *World Today*, Australian ABC, June 2, 2000)

Merely satisfying customers will not be enough to earn their loyalty. Instead, they must experience exceptional service worthy of their repeat business and referral. Understand the factors that drive this customer revolution.

—Rick Tate, author and customer-loyalty strategist

———

Customer-centricity should be about delivering value for customers that will eventually create value for the company.

—Robert G. Thompson, author (from his book *Hooked on Customers: The Five Habits of Legendary Customer-Centric Companies*, 2014)

———

When leaders reframe customers into guests, and results into experiences, profits escalate.

—Eric Schiffer, author and entrepreneur

Unless you have 100% customer satisfaction . . . you must improve.

—Horst Schulze, president of the Ritz Carlton Hotels

———❖———

The purpose of a business is to create a customer who creates customers.

—Shiv Singh, senior brand executive, Visa Inc.

———❖———

It starts with respect. If you respect the customer as a human being, and truly honor their right to be treated fairly and honestly, everything else is much easier.

—Doug Smith, author and team-building expert

Never leave your customers wondering.

—Kevin Stirtz, author and web marketing consultant

———◆———

Until you understand your customers—deeply and genuinely—you cannot truly serve them.

—Rasheed Ogunlaru, life coach, speaker, and author (from his book *Soul Trader: Putting the Heart Back into Your Business*, 2012)

———◆———

The single most important thing to remember about any enterprise is that there are no results inside its walls. The result of a business is a satisfied customer.

—Peter F. Drucker, management consultant, educator, and author

Courteous treatment will make a customer a walking advertisement.

—J. C. Penney, founder of retail chain JCPenney

———◆———

Spend a lot of time talking to customers face to face. You'd be amazed how many companies don't listen to their customers.

—Ross Perot, businessman and Reform Party presidential candidate

———◆———

Customers don't expect you to be perfect. They do expect you to fix things when they go wrong.

—Donald Porter, British Airways executive

No customer walks into your business, gives you money and then says, "dissatisfy me, please." Aim for 100% customer satisfaction.

—Bill Quiseng, writer, speaker, hotel executive, and
blogger (from billquiseng.com)

Never say no when a client asks for something—even if it is the moon. You can always try, and anyhow there is plenty of time afterward to explain that it was not possible.

—César Ritz, founder of the Hôtel Ritz (Paris) and
The Ritz Hotel (London)

We should never be allowed to forget that it is the customer who, in the end, determines how many people are employed and what sort of wages companies can afford.

—Lord Robens, chairman of National Coal Board,
United Kingdom

The more you engage with customers, the clearer things become and the easier it is to determine what you should be doing.

—John Russell, president of Harley Davidson, Europe

⸻◆⸻

Service, in short, is not what you do, but who you are. It is a way of living that you need to bring to everything you do, if you are to bring it to your customer interactions.

—Betsy Sanders, Nordstrom executive and author (from her book *Fabled Service: Ordinary Acts, Extraordinary Outcomes*, 1995)

⸻◆⸻

Every company's greatest assets are its customers, because without customers there is no company.

—Michael LeBoeuf, business professor and author

Southwest Airlines is successful because the company understands it's a customer service company. It also happens to be an airline.

—Harvey Mackay, author and founder of MackayMitchell Envelope Co. (from *Inc.* magazine, April 17, 2012)

⟨⟩

For us, our most important stakeholder is not our stockholders, it is our customers. We're in business to serve the needs and desires of our core customer base.

—John Mackey, cofounder and CEO of Whole Foods Market

⟨⟩

The simple act of saying "thank you" is a demonstration of gratitude in response to an experience that was meaningful to a customer or citizen.

—Simon Mainwaring, branding consultant, advertising executive, and social media guru (from his book *We First: How Brands and Consumers Use Social Media to Build a Better World*, 2011)

The golden rule for every businessman is this: Put yourself in your customer's place.

—Orison Swett Marden, inspirational author and founder of *SUCCESS* magazine

---

You are serving a customer, not a life sentence. Learn how to enjoy your work.

—Laurie McIntosh, facilitator, writer, and editor for *Business Training Works* (from her book *A Mixed Bunch: 21 Cases of Diversity Training*, 2009)

A sale is made on every call you make. Either you sell the client some stock or he sells you a reason he can't. Either way a sale is made, the only question is who is gonna close?

—Jim Young, fictional character in the movie *Boiler Room*

Customer service is seldom about the customer; it is usually about the seller's chances of making more money from that customer in future.

—Mokokoma Mokhonoana, philosopher, social critic, graphic designer, and writer

Customer conversion is dependent on the right customer conversation.

—Rasheed Ogunlaru, life coach, speaker, and author (from his book *Soul Trader: Putting the Heart Back into Your Business*, 2012)

Whether you are big or small, you cannot give good customer service if your employees don't feel good about coming to work.

—Martin Oliver, executive with Kwik-Fit Financial Service

Make your customers comfortable and they will give you their lives.

—Paul Orfalea, founder of Kinko's (from his book *Copy This!: Lessons from a Hyperactive Dyslexic Who Turned a Bright Idea into One of America's Best Companies*, 2005)

A courteous, creative initial contact with the customer can go a long way to promote sales. If a customer has to wait for you say, "I'll be with you in a moment." Such actions will reduce the number of customers who leave without being served. When you are free to help the waiting customer, your initial comment should be, "Thank you for waiting."

—Peter J. Patsula, author and founder of Patsula Media (from his online publication *The Entrepreneur's Guidebook Series*)

I don't like customer service, because I don't believe the customer should have to pay and help out too.

—Jarod Kintz, author

I always look each person squarely in the eyes and whenever possible, try to say something personal. It might be only a comment such as "I love your hair," or "What a beautiful dress you're wearing," but I give each person my undivided attention, and I don't allow anything to distract me. Each person whose hand I shake is the most important person in the world at that moment.

—Mary Kay Ash, founder of Mary Kay Cosmetics

When you are skinning your customers, you should leave some skin on to grow so that you can skin them again.

—Nikita Khrushchev, Soviet leader (from *British Business News*, 1961)

Branding is not merely about differentiating products; it is about striking emotional chords with consumers. It is about cultivating identity, attachment, and trust to inspire customer loyalty.

—Nirmalya Kumar, professor of marketing and director of Aditya Birla India Centre, London Business School (from huffingtonpost.com, June 20, 2013)

Successful entrepreneurship begins and ends with customer wants and needs, not what you want and need.
—Joseph C. Kunz Jr., entrepreneur and author

Quality in a service or product is not what you put into it. It is what the client or customer gets out of it.
—Peter F. Drucker, management consultant, educator, and author

A satisfied customer is the best business strategy of all.
—Michael LeBoeuf, business professor and author

Rule 1: The customer is always right. Rule 2: If the customer is ever wrong, reread Rule 1.

—Stew Leonard, retailer

The true purpose of a business is to create and keep a customer, not to make you money.

—Theodore Levitt, economist, professor at Harvard Business School, and author

Capitalize on charm by continually captivating your customer.

—Ryan Lilly, business incubation professional and author

When the customer comes first, the customer will last.

    —Robert Half, founder of Robert Half International

<hr/>

When people talk about successful retailers and those that are not so successful, the customer determines at the end of the day who is successful and for what reason.

    —Jerry Harvey, cofounder of Australia retailing chain Harvey Norman Holdings (from interview with Slovenia magazine *Ljubljana Life,* August 2002)

<hr/>

The purpose of every business and organization is to get and keep customers.

    —Theodore Levitt, economist, professor at Harvard Business School, and author (from his book *The Marketing Imagination,* 1986)

The buyer needs a hundred eyes; the seller but one.

—Italian proverb

***

In the United States, you say the customer is always right. In Japan, we say the customer is God. There is a big difference.

—Japanese businessman

***

Our DNA is as a consumer company—for that individual customer who's voting thumbs up or thumbs down. That's who we think about. And we think that our job is to take responsibility for the complete user experience. And if it's not up to par, it's our fault, plain and simply.

—Steve Jobs, cofounder of Apple and Pixar Animation
(from *Fortune* magazine, March 7, 2008)

Customers love certainty; make sure you give it to them.

—Amit Kalantri, author

———◆———

A complaint is a unique opportunity to strengthen the relationship with the client.

—Kevin Kelly, author (from his book *DO! The Pursuit of Xceptional Execution*, 2013)

———◆———

It is not the employer who pays the wages. Employers only handle the money. It is the customer who pays the wages.

—Henry Ford, founder of Ford Motor Co. (from Ford Motors PR compilation)

The question is, then, do we try to make things easy on ourselves or do we try to make things easy on our customers, whoever they may be?

—Erwin Fran, author

There are more fools among buyers than among sellers.

—French Proverb

You'll never have a product or price advantage again. They can be easily duplicated, but a strong customer service culture can't be copied.

—Jerry Fritz, director of Management Institute University of Wisconsin

Our belief was that if we kept putting great products in front of customers, they would continue to open their wallets.

—Steve Jobs, cofounder of Apple and Pixar Animation (from *Success* magazine, June 2010)

We see our customers as invited guests to a party, and we are the hosts.

—Jeff Bezos, founder of Amazon.com

Your most unhappy customers are your greatest source of learning.

—Bill Gates, cofounder of Microsoft

The goal as a company is to have customer service that is not just the best but legendary.

—Sam Walton, founder of Wal-Mart

If you don't genuinely like your customers, chances are they won't buy.

—Thomas Watson, chairman and CEO of IBM

Customer satisfaction is worthless. Customer loyalty is priceless.

—Jeffrey Gitomer, author (from his book *Customer Satisfaction Is Worthless, Customer Loyalty Is Priceless: How to Make Customers Love You, Keep Them Coming Back and Tell Everyone They Know*, 1998)

People rarely buy what they need. They buy what they want.

—Seth Godin, author, entrepreneur, and public speaker

———◆———

Customer service is just a day-in, day-out ongoing, never ending, unremitting, persevering, compassionate type of activity.

—Leon Gorman, chairman of L. L. Bean

———◆———

The customer experience is the next competitive battleground.

—Jerry Gregoire, chief information officer, Dell Computer

If you make the customer a promise . . . make sure you deliver on it.

> —Merv Griffin, talk show host, entertainer, and media mogul

———◆◆———

Dealing with people is probably the biggest problem you face, especially if you are in business. Yes, and that is also true if you are a housewife, architect, or engineer.

> —Dale Carnegie, writer, lecturer, and developer of self-improvement courses

———◆◆———

Instead of focusing on the competition, focus on the customer.

> —Scott Cook, founder of Intuit Inc.

It is so much easier to be nice, to be respectful, to put yourself in your customers' shoes and try to understand how you might help them before they ask for help, than it is to try to mend a broken customer relationship.

> —Mark Cuban, owner of Dallas Mavericks, Landmark Theatres, and Magnolia Pictures

---

Friendly makes sales—and friendly generates repeat business.

> —Jeffrey Gitomer, author

The longer you wait, the harder it is to produce outstanding customer service.

> —William H. Davidow, high-technology industry executive and venture capitalist

Profit in business comes from repeat customers; customers that boast about your product and service, and that bring friends with them.

—W. Edwards Deming, engineer, scholar, author, and management consultant

———

Right or wrong, the customer is always right.

—Marshall Field, founder of Marshall Field department store

———

Letting your customers set your standards is a dangerous game, because the race to the bottom is pretty easy to win. Setting your own standards—and living up to them—is a better way to profit. Not to mention a better way to make your day worth all the effort you put into it.

—Seth Godin, author, entrepreneur, and public speaker (from his blog sethgodin.typepad.com, July 28, 2006)

If you make customers unhappy in the physical world, they might each tell 6 friends. If you make customers unhappy on the Internet, they can each tell 6,000 friends.

—Jeff Bezos, founder of Amazon.com

———◆———

Anything a customer can do for themselves is where service stops and relevance begins.

—Jim Blasingame, author

———◆———

Here is a simple but powerful rule: always give people more than what they expect to get.

—Nelson Boswell, self-help author

Make your product easier to buy than your competition, or you will find your customers buying from them, not you.

—Mark Cuban, owner of Dallas Mavericks, Landmark Theatres, and Magnolia Pictures

———◆———

The aim of marketing is to know and understand the customer so well the product or service fits him and sells itself.

—Peter F. Drucker, management consultant, educator, and author

———◆———

I have always believed that the way you treat your employees is the way they will treat your customers, and that people flourish when they are praised.

—Sir Richard Branson, billionaire entrepreneur and founder of Virgin Airlines

The best customer service is if the customer doesn't need to call you, doesn't need to talk to you. It just works.

—Jeff Bezos, founder of Amazon.com

<hr>

The better you understand your customer, the higher the probability of success.

—Diane Bryant, Intel Corp. executive

<hr>

Don't try to tell the customer what he wants. If you want to be smart, be smart in the shower. Then get out, go to work and serve the customer!

—Gene Buckley, president of Sikorsky Aircraft

If you're not serving the customer, your job is to be serving someone who is.
—Jan Carlzon, CEO of SAS

———❖———

Customer service is not a department, it's everyone's job.
—Anonymous

———❖———

We don't want to push our ideas on to customers, we simply want to make what they want.
—Laura Ashley, fashion designer

———❖———

Make a customer, not a sale.
—Katherine Barchetti, founder of K. Barchetti Shops, Pittsburgh

If you wish to prosper, let your customer prosper.

> —Frederic Bastiat, French liberal theorist, legislator, and political economist

<hr/>

Loyal customers, they don't just come back, they don't simply recommend you, they insist that their friends do business with you.

> —Chip Bell, founder of Chip Bell Group

<hr/>

If we can keep our competitors focused on us while we stay focused on the customer, ultimately we'll turn out all right.

> —Jeff Bezos, founder of Amazon.com

I am the world's worst salesman; therefore, I must make it easy for people to buy.

— F. W. Woolworth, founder of five-and-dime chain

In the end, the customer doesn't know, or care, if you are small or large as an organization. . . . She or he only focuses on the garment hanging on the rail in the store.

— Giorgio Armani, fashion designer

Pretend that every single person you meet has a sign around his or her neck that says, "Make me feel important." Not only will you succeed in sales, you will succeed in life.

— Mary Kay Ash, founder of Mary Kay Cosmetics

I think one purpose is very clear among corporations and business leaders: make profits, deliver high return for stockholders, conquer markets, service consumers and create jobs. But in today's world, demands from corporations and leaders are much more than that. We need to understand what people really want at the very end.

—Vicente Fox, President of Mexico (from interview with XL Alliance in July 2011 at the Hispanic Retail 360 Summit)

Do what you do so well that they will want to see it again and bring their friends.

—Walt Disney, founder of Walt Disney Studio and theme parks

Never treat your audience as customers, always as partners.

—Jimmy Stewart, actor

Passion

Many successful companies were the unintended consequence of a founder indulging his passion. A prominent example is General Electric, whose origins in the late 1800s flowed directly from founder Thomas Edison's zealous preoccupation with inventing the incandescent lamp. A 13-year-old passionate hobbyist programmer named Bill Gates grew up to cofound Microsoft and become the world's richest person. Benjamin Franklin, a multifaceted hobbyist, parlayed his passion for reading into a thriving career as a printer. The poet Robert Frost, like so many of the quotable luminaries below, illuminated the link between passion and business achievement when he said, "My goal in life is to unite my avocation with my vocation, as my two eyes make one in sight."

If your energy is as boundless as your ambition, total commitment may be a way of life you should seriously consider.

> —Joyce Brothers, psychologist and advice columnist (from her book *Positive Plus: The Practical Plan for Liking Yourself Better*)

❖

Seek out that particular mental attribute which makes you feel most deeply and vitally alive, along with which comes the inner voice which says, "This is the real me," and when you have found that attitude, follow it.

> —William James, philosopher and psychologist (from his book *The Principles of Psychology*, 1890)

❖

Be Shameless. Experiment. This is the only way to identify your true passion.

> —Vishwas Mudagal, entrepreneur and author (from his book *Losing My Religion*, 2014)

Get in touch with your passion and put it to work at work.

—Marilyn Suttle, author and motivational speaker

———◆———

I have always pursued everything I was interested in with a true passion—some would say obsession—to win. I've always held the bar pretty high for myself: I've set extremely high personal goals.

—Sam Walton, founder of Wal-Mart

———◆———

If you love what you do and are willing to do what it takes, it's within your reach. And it'll be worth every minute you spend alone at night, thinking and thinking about what it is you want to design or build.

—Steve Wozniak, inventor and cofounder of Apple Inc.

Love what you are doing because that's the only way you'll ever be really good at it.

—Fred Trump, real estate developer

———◆———

Passion is energy. Feel the power that comes from focusing on what excites you.

—Oprah Winfrey, media mogul, television host, and actress

———◆———

It's almost embarrassing to admit this, but it's true: there hasn't been a day in my adult life when I haven't spent some time thinking about merchandising.

—Sam Walton, founder of Wal-Mart (from his book *Sam Walton: Made in America*, 1992)

Your work is going to fill a large part of your life, and the only way to be truly satisfied is to do what you believe is great work. And the only way to do great work is to love what you do.

—Steve Jobs, cofounder of Apple and Pixar Animation (from his 2005 commencement address at Stanford University)

———◆———

True art is characterized by an irresistible urge in the creative artist.

—Albert Einstein, developer of the theory of relativity, discussing musician Ernst Bloch in 1950

———◆———

Nothing is so contagious as enthusiasm.

—Edward George Bulwer Lytton, novelist (from *The Last Days of Pompeii*, 1834)

What makes an entrepreneur is not knowing everything about business, but rather being passionate and fearless.

—Rehan Choudhry, founder of Life is Beautiful Festival and speaker (from article "The Best Business Advice You'll Ever Get," *Entrepreneur,* July 2, 2014)

Geeks are people who love something so much that all the details matter.

—Marissa Mayer, CEO of Yahoo!

Disneyland is a work of love. We didn't go into Disneyland just with the idea of making money.

—Walt Disney, founder of Walt Disney Studio and theme parks

If you always do what interests you, at least one person is pleased.

—Katharine Hepburn, actress

——◆——

I never did a day's work in my life. It was all fun.

—Thomas Edison, inventor

——◆——

Money was never a big motivation for me, except as a way to keep score. The real excitement is playing the game.

—Donald Trump, real estate developer, author, and presidential candidate (from his book *Trump: The Art of the Deal*, 1987)

Nothing great was ever achieved without enthusiasm.

> —Ralph Waldo Emerson, philosopher, poet, and essayist

Some people find an interest in making money, and though they appear to be slaving, many actually enjoy every minute of their work.

> —Walter Annenberg, publisher

Enthusiasm is the sparkle in your eyes, the swing in your gait, the grip of your hand. The irresistible surge of will and energy to execute your ideas.

> —Henry Ford, founder of Ford Motor Co.

No one has a greater asset for his business than a man's pride in his work.

—Mary Parker Follett, business thinker and author
(from her book *Freedom and Co-ordination*, 1949)

———◆———

It takes a deep commitment to change and an even deeper commitment to grow.

—Ralph Ellison, novelist

———◆———

It had long since come to my attention that people of accomplishment rarely sat back and let things happen to them. They went out and happened to things.

—Leonardo Da Vinci, artist

If you genuinely want something, don't wait for it—teach yourself to be impatient.

> —Gurbaksh Chahal, entrepreneur and author (from his book *The Dream: How I Learned the Risks and Rewards of Entrepreneurship and Made Millions,* 2008)

Give yourself an even greater challenge than the one you are trying to master and you will develop the powers necessary to overcome the original difficulty.

> —William J. Bennett, US secretary of education (from his book *The Book of Virtues,* 1993)

Only one who devotes himself to a cause with his whole strength and soul can be a true master. For this reason, mastery demands all of a person.

> —Albert Einstein, developer of the theory of relativity

The trick is in what one emphasizes. We either make ourselves miserable, or we make ourselves strong. The amount of work is the same.

—Carlos Castaneda, author (from his book *Journey to Ixtian: The Lessons of Don Juan*, 1972)

I get to do what I like to do every single day of the year.

—Warren Buffett, legendary investor and CEO of Berkshire Hathaway

Success comes to those who dedicate everything to their passion in life. To be successful, it is also very important to be humble and never let fame or money travel to your head.

—A. R. Rahman, musician

To succeed . . . you need to find something to hold on to, something to motivate you, something to inspire you.

—Tony Dorsett, NFL football player

———◆·◆———

Passion is the single most powerful competitive advantage an organization can claim in building its success.

—Richard Y. Chang, consultant and author (from his book *The Passion Plan at Work: Building a Passion-Driven Organization*, 2001)

———◆·◆———

Success isn't guaranteed, but failure is certain if you aren't truly emotionally invested in your work.

—Biz Stone, cofounder of Twitter (from his book *Things a Little Bird Told Me: Confessions of the Creative Mind*, 2014)

Deals are my art form. Other people paint beautifully on canvas or write wonderful poetry. I like making deals, preferably big deals. That's how I get my kicks.

—Donald Trump, real estate developer, author, and presidential candidate (from his book *Trump: The Art of the Deal,* 1987)

———◆◆———

I'm not really interested in making money.

—Steven Spielberg, filmmaker

———◆◆———

We are told that talent creates its own opportunities. But it sometimes seems that intense desire creates not only its own opportunities, but its own talents.

—Eric Hoffer, philosopher (from his book *The Passionate State of Mind,* 1955)

As long as the mind can envision the fact that you can do something, you can do it, as long as you really believe 100 percent.

—Arnold Schwarzenegger, actor and governor of California

———◆———

The road to happiness lies in two simple principles: find what interests you and that you can do well, and put your whole soul into it—every bit of energy and ambition and natural ability you have.

—John D. Rockefeller, industrialist, cofounder of Standard Oil Co., and philanthropist

———◆———

We may affirm that nothing great in the world has been accomplished without passion.

—Georg Wilhelm Friedrich Hegel, philosopher (from his book *The Philosophy of History*, 1900)

To accomplish great things, we must not only act but also dream, not only plan but also believe.

    —Anatole France, poet and journalist

———◆———

A man can succeed at almost anything for which he has unlimited enthusiasm.

    —Charles M. Schwab, steel magnate

———◆———

People are always good company when they are doing what they really enjoy.

    —Samuel Butler, novelist

Success is not the key to happiness. Happiness is the key to success. If you love what you are doing, you will be successful.

—Albert Schweitzer, theologian and philosopher

Nothing is so contagious as enthusiasm.

—Samuel Taylor Coleridge, poet and philosopher

No one has a greater asset for his business than a man's pride in his work.

—Mary Parker Follett, social worker, management consultant, and philosopher (from her book *Freedom and Coordination*, 1949)

Only he is successful in his business who makes that pursuit which affords him the highest pleasure sustain him.

> —Henry David Thoreau, author, poet, philosopher, abolitionist, and naturalist

Successful and unsuccessful people do not vary greatly in their abilities. They vary in their desires to reach their potential.

> —John C. Maxwell, author, speaker, and pastor

To be successful, you have to have your heart in your business, and your business in your heart.

> —Thomas J. Watson, chairman and CEO of IBM

Ambition is a dream with a V8 engine.

> —Elvis Presley, musician

Wisdom

Exactly what constitutes wisdom? What are its constituent parts? The *Oxford English Dictionary* defines it like this: "The capacity of judging rightly in matters relating to life and conduct; soundness of judgment in the choice between means and ends; sometimes less strictly, sound sense in practical affairs; opposite to folly." In the context of business, particularly within complex organizations, wisdom is an especially abstruse quality to assess, given the many variables around which wisdom must be applied. Leaders are called upon to make sound decisions and exercise correct judgments concerning customers, employees, shareholders, regulators, and rivals. The quotes that follow reflect all kinds of wisdom across the business spectrum.

Wisdom is not like money to be tied up and hidden.
—Akan proverb

———◆———

. . . in the end, it is impossible to have a great life unless it is a meaningful life. And it is very difficult to have a meaningful life without meaningful work. Perhaps, then, you might gain that rare tranquility that comes from knowing that you've had a hand in creating something of intrinsic excellence that makes a contribution. Indeed, you might even gain that deepest of all satisfactions: knowing that your short time here on this earth has been well spent, and that it mattered.
—Jim Collins, business consultant, author, and lecturer

———◆———

The most important single central fact about a free market is that no exchange takes place unless both parties benefit.
—Milton Friedman, economist

Beware of little expenses; a small leak will sink a great ship.

—Benjamin Franklin, US founding father and inventor

———◆———

Retirement is the menopause of an employee's mind and hands.

—Mokokoma Mokhonoana, philosopher, social critic,
graphic designer, and writer

———◆———

A little learning is a dangerous thing. Drink deep. . . .

—Alexander Pope, English poet

143

Being BIG is no good if your foundation is weak. A giant with skinny legs is an invitation to be tripped.

—Peter J. Patsula, founder of Patsula Media and author

The first one gets the oyster, the second gets the shell.

—Andrew Carnegie, steel industrialist

Without involvement, there is no commitment. Mark it down, asterisk it, circle it, underline it.

—Stephen Covey, educator, author, and businessman

144

In the moment of crisis, the wise build bridges and the foolish build dams.

—Nigerian proverb

If you see a bandwagon, it's too late.

—James Goldsmith, Anglo-French billionaire financier

Stay away from hedge funds unless you are very wealthy and financially sophisticated.

—Tom Ajamie and Bruce Kelly, coauthors of *Financial Serial Killers: Inside the World of Wall Street Money Hustlers, Swindlers, and Con Men*, 2010

Knowledge has no value except that which can be gained from its application toward some worthy end.

> —Napoleon Hill, pioneer of the modern genre of personal success

———◆———

Reality is merely an illusion, albeit a very persistent one.

> —Albert Einstein, developer of the theory of relativity

———◆———

The true price of anything you do is the amount of time you exchange for it.

> —Henry David Thoreau, author, poet, philosopher, abolitionist, and naturalist

Never give up on a dream just because of the time it will take to accomplish it. The time will pass anyway.

—Earl Nightingale, radio personality and writer

There is nothing more frightful than ignorance in action.

— Johann Wolfgang von Goethe, German writer and statesman

A hard beginning maketh a good ending.

—John Heywood, English playwright

The bottom line is down where it belongs—at the bottom.

—Paul Hawken, environmentalist, entrepreneur, author, and activist

A moment's insight is sometimes worth a life's experience.

—Oliver Wendell Holmes, US Supreme Court justice

Nothing is a mistake. There's no win and no fail. There's only make.

—Corita Kent, Catholic nun, artist, and educator

One finds limits by pushing them.

—Herbert Simon, political scientist and economist

The toe you step on today may be the ass you have to kiss tomorrow. So be careful!

—Nick Lyons, teacher, writer, and publisher

All you have to do is know where you're going.

—Earl Nightingale, radio personality and writer

The habit of always putting off an experience until you can afford it, or until the time is right, or until you know how to do it is one of the greatest burglars of joy. Be deliberate, but once you've made up your mind—jump in.

> —Charles R. Swindoll, evangelical Christian pastor, author, educator, and radio preacher

Do not worry if you have built your castles in the air. They are where they should be. Now put the foundations under them.

> —Henry David Thoreau, author, poet, philosopher, abolitionist, and naturalist

I like thinking big. If you're going to be thinking anything, you might as well think big.

> —Donald Trump, real estate developer, author, and presidential candidate

Twenty years from now you will be more disappointed by the things that you didn't do than by the ones you did do.

—Mark Twain, author and humorist

———◆———

Don't take another mouthful before you have swallowed what is in your mouth.

—Malagasy proverb

———◆———

Do you want to flourish in the garden of life? Life's gardeners pluck the weeds and care only for the productive plants.

—Bryant McGill, author

151

Great is the art of beginning, but greater is the art of ending.

—Henry Wadsworth Longfellow, poet

———◆———

Quality is never an accident; it is always the result of high intention, sincere effort, intelligent direction and skillful execution; it represents the wise choice of many alternatives.

—William A. Foster, World War II era Medal of Honor awardee

———◆———

Diligence is the mother of good luck.

—Benjamin Franklin, US founding father and inventor

I will demand a commitment to excellence and to victory, and that is what life is all about.

—Vince Lombardi, professional football coaching legend

———◆———

Depend on the rabbit's foot if you will, but remember it didn't work for the rabbit.

—R. E. Shay, humorist

———◆———

It's not what you do, but what you appear to do.

—James Pritchert, author

Community organizing is all about building grassroots support. It's about identifying the people around you with whom you can create a common, passionate cause. And it's about ignoring the conventional wisdom of company politics and instead playing the game by very different rules.

—Tom Peters, author and business management expert

Often-times the most difficult competition comes, not from the strong, the intelligent, the conservative competitor, but from the man who is holding on by the eyelids and is ignorant of his costs, and anyway he's got to keep running or bust!

—John D. Rockefeller, industrialist, cofounder of
Standard Oil Co., and philanthropist

It is the greatest of all advantages to enjoy no advantage at all.

—Henry David Thoreau, author, poet, philosopher,
abolitionist, and naturalist

People expect a certain reaction from a business, and when you pleasantly exceed those expectations, you've somehow passed an important psychological threshold.

—Richard Thalheimer, founder, CEO, and chairman of the Sharper Image Corp.

On every level of life, from housework to heights of prayer, in all judgment and efforts to get things done, hurry and impatience are sure marks of the amateur.

—Evelyn Underhill, English Anglo-Catholic writer and pacifist

In the end, you are measured not by how much you undertake but by what you finally accomplished.

—Donald Trump, real estate developer, author, and presidential candidate

If you try to look too far down the road that stretches mysteriously into the future, you're liable to trip on a rock; if you look just past your toes, you'll miss the bear—always hungry, licking his lips—waiting eagerly for you. . . .

> —Nick Lyons, teacher, writer, and publisher

Sometimes the biggest gain in productive energy will come from cleaning the cobwebs, dealing with old business, and clearing the desks—cutting loose debris that's impeding forward motion.

> —David Allen, author

Waiting is a trap. There will always be reasons to wait. The truth is, there are only two things in life, reasons and results, and reasons simply don't count.

> —Robert Anthony, author and psychologist

There is a light at the end of the tunnel, but the way out is through.

—David Allen, author

———◆———

Each indecision brings its own delays and days are lost lamenting over lost days. . . .

— Johann Wolfgang von Goethe, German writer and statesman

———◆———

Never mistake motion for action.

—Ernest Hemingway, novelist

Knowledge without wisdom is like water in the sand.
—Guinean proverb

Simplicity boils down to two steps: Identify the essential. Eliminate the rest.
—Leo Babauta, author

The difference between perseverance and obstinacy is that one often comes from a strong will, and the other from a strong won't.
—Henry Ward Beecher, Congregationalist clergyman and social reformer

Well done is better than well said.

—Benjamin Franklin, US founding father and inventor

When you're working and making money, that's all good, but there has to be something that provides a substance, I think.

—Mekhi Phifer, actor

The avoidance of taxes is the only intellectual pursuit that still carries any reward.

—John Maynard Keynes, economist

Price is what you pay. Value is what you get.
— Warren Buffett, legendary investor and CEO of
  Berkshire Hathaway

———◆———

It is my belief that tax credits only go to people who are making money, and they generally keep it.
— Diane Feinstein, US senator

———◆———

There is no quick way of making money. People come to you with tips for the races or offer the latest Ponzi scheme, but I can see them coming a mile off. I just go with the adage that if it sounds too good to be true it probably is.
— Wilbur Smith, novelist

All business proceeds on beliefs, or judgments of probabilities, and not on certainties.

—Charles W. Eliot, Harvard University president

<hr/>

Prophecy is a good line of business, but it is full of risks.

—Mark Twain, author and humorist

<hr/>

If something is wrong outside the realm of business, then it's wrong inside the realm of business.

—Ken Iverson, author

The borrower is slave to the lender and the debtor to the creditor.

—Benjamin Franklin, US founding father and inventor

True wealth is the harmonious coexistence of all there is, was and ever shall be. It is a combination of self-determination, self-expression, self-realization and complete unreserved love for humanity, life and the universe. It is also, unfortunately, a sucker's trap— its reality infinitely intangible, its possession as feasible as playing hopscotch on the shadows of Jupiter.

—Peter J. Patsula, founder of Patsula Media and author

Seven deadly sins: politics without principle; wealth without work; pleasure without conscience; knowledge without character; business without morality; science without humanity; and worship without sacrifice.

—E. Stanley Jones, author and Methodist Christian missionary and theologian

Note to the wise: whenever someone insists that he wants to buy something from you, but tells you there's no real value in it yet, two things are happening: he's lying, and you're being taken.

 —Mike Stackpole, science fiction author

———◆———

The difference between tax avoidance and tax evasion is the thickness of a prison wall.

 —Denis Healey, motivational speaker, writer, and
  consultant

———◆———

Honesty is the first chapter in the book of wisdom.

 —Thomas Jefferson, US founding father and president

The problem with the rat race is that even if you win, you're still a rat.

—Lily Tomlin, actress and comedian

Achievement results from work realizing ambition.

—Adam Ant, musician

Always consider who you're learning from. Don't listen to people who are not experiencing the success you want.

—Ehab Atalla, author, entrepreneur, and investor

Nothing truly valuable arises from ambition or from a mere sense of duty; it stems rather from love and devotion towards men and towards objective things.

—Albert Einstein, developer of the theory of relativity

Wisdom is knowing what to do next, skill is knowing how to do it, and virtue is doing it.

—David Starr Jordan, ichthyologist, educator, eugenicist, and peace activist

More business is lost every year through neglect than through any other cause.

—Rose F. Kennedy, Kennedy family matriarch

One who causes others misfortune also teaches them wisdom.

—African proverb

———◆———

Wisdom does not come overnight.

—Somali proverb

———◆———

Never compete with someone who has nothing to lose.

—Baltasar Gracián, Spanish Jesuit author

I think everybody should get rich and famous and do everything they ever dreamed of so they can see that it's not the answer.

—Jim Carrey, actor and comedian

In modern business it is not the crook who is to be feared most, it is the honest man who doesn't know what he is doing.

—Pablo Casals, Spanish cellist

Method is the very hinge of business, and there is no method without punctuality.

—Richard Cecil, Evangelical Anglican priest

The greatest power is often simple patience.
　　—E. Joseph Cossman, marketing impresario and
　　author

The wise learn many things from their enemies.
　　—Aristophanes, Greek playwright

Showing up is important and it is a big part of becoming successful.
　　—Andy Albright, author

Every business, like a painting, operates according to its own rules. There are many ways to run a successful company. What works once may never work again. What everyone tells you never to do may just work, once.

—Sir Richard Branson, billionaire entrepreneur and founder of Virgin Airlines

You only have to do a very few things right in your life so long as you don't do too many things wrong.

—Warren Buffett, legendary investor and CEO of Berkshire Hathaway

For a successful technology, reality must take precedence over public relations, for Nature cannot be fooled.

—Richard P. Feynman, physicist and winner of the Nobel Prize in Physics

Those who say it can not be done, should not interrupt those doing it.

—Chinese proverb

⸺◆⸺

The most efficient route that nature has found from point A to point B is rarely a straight line. It is always the path of least resistance.

—Mark Buckingham and Curt Coffman, coauthors of *First, Break All the Rules,* 1999

⸺◆⸺

Everything should be made as simple as possible, but not simpler.

—Albert Einstein, developer of the theory of relativity

The man who will use his skill and constructive imagination to see how much he can give for a dollar, instead of how little he can give for a dollar, is bound to succeed.

—Henry Ford, founder of Ford Motor Co.

———◆———

The only way around is through.

—Robert Frost, poet

———◆———

The secret of business is to know something nobody else knows.

—Aristotle Onassis, Greek shipping magnate

Business is a game, played for fantastic stakes, and you're in competition with experts. If you want to win, you have to learn to be a master of the game.

—Sidney Sheldon, author

<hr/>

What is it that you like doing? If you don't like it, get out of it, because you'll be lousy at it. You don't have to stay with a job for the rest of your life, because if you don't like it you'll never be successful in it.

—Lee Iacocca, chairman and CEO of Chrysler Motors

<hr/>

To think is easy. To act is difficult. To act as one thinks is the most difficult.

—Johann Wolfgang von Goethe, German writer and statesman

If we can just take a few companies, and use those as models, as examples, to show the rest of corporate America how they can become more competitive, that's what I'd like to do and that's what I hope to do.

>—Henry Kravis, cofounder of Kohlberg Kravis Roberts & Co.

Age is only a number, a cipher for the records. A man can't retire his experience. He must use it. Experience achieves more with less energy and time.

>—Bernard Baruch, financier, stock investor, philanthropist, and statesman

I believe that you have to plan your retirement, not by thinking that you will be deprived of something, but rather that something will be added to your life. You see, you do not start from zero, you are rich with the totality of experience that life has given to you. The past years are like a crown which you wear at the beginning of the next phase of your life.

>— Colonel Sanders, founder of Kentucky Fried Chicken

The best way of learning about anything is by doing.

—Sir Richard Branson, billionaire entrepreneur and founder of Virgin Airlines

———⊱⬥⬥⬥⬦⬦⬦⬥⬥⬥⬦———

The passage ahead looms as a perilous one. But when I think how far we have travelled, I feel confident the difficulties ahead will be overcome.

—Bernard Baruch, financier, stock investor, philanthropist, and statesman (from the *Indianapolis Star*, February 13, 1958)

———⊱⬥⬥⬥⬦⬦⬦⬥⬥⬥⬦———

When a person with experience meets a person with money, pretty soon, the person with the experience will have the money and the person with the money will have the experience.

—Estée Lauder, cofounder of Estée Lauder Companies

In the business world, the rearview mirror is always clearer than the windshield.

> —Warren Buffett, legendary investor and CEO of Berkshire Hathaway

———◆◆———

In the business world, everyone is paid in two coins: cash and experience. Take the experience first; the cash will come later.

> —Harold Geneen, chairman of ITT Corp.

———◆◆———

I can walk through the front door of any factory and out the back and tell you if it's making money or not. I can just tell by the way it's being run and by the spirit of the workers.

> —Harvey S. Firestone, founder of Firestone Tire and Rubber Co.

No matter how bright someone is, nothing beats experience. And that takes time. There is no quick fix, no five easy steps.

—Tony Fernandes, entrepreneur

———◆———

Men intrinsically do not trust new things that they have not experienced themselves.

—Machiavelli, Italian Renaissance political philosopher (from his book *The Prince*, 1515)

———◆———

Women attribute their success to hard work, luck, and help from other people. Men will attribute . . . whatever success they have . . . to their own core skills.

—Sheryl Sandberg, chief operating officer of Facebook

Only so much I know as I have lived.

> —Ralph Waldo Emerson, essayist, lecturer, and poet
> (from his book *The Essential Writings of Ralph Waldo
> Emerson*, edited by Brooks Atkinson, 2000)

Winners take time to relish their work, knowing that scaling the mountain is what makes the view from the top so exhilarating.

> —Denis Waitley, motivational speaker, writer, and
> consultant

In short, learn everything you can. In business, what you don't know can hurt you.

> —Peter J. Patsula, founder of Patsula Media and author

Profit, Money, and Greed

Money can be used for good and bad. Corporations need to make a profit to stay in business, and employees need to be sufficiently paid in order to keep working. But at some point, accumulating money stops being a productive incentive and morphs into greed. This fault line surely predates the "robber barons" who emerged during the Industrial Revolution. To a widening segment of the population, yesteryear's robber barons are today's "one-percenters"—hedge fund billionaires and Wall Street CEOs. And now, the "greed-is-good" zeitgeist of the late twentieth century has given way to the Occupy Wall Street movement and the Bernie Sanders presidential campaign—twenty-first-century developments fueled by wide economic disparity and income inequality. The following quotes convey all these perspectives on money within the economic sphere.

A corporation's primary goal is to make money. Government's primary role is to take a big chunk of that money and give it to others.

—Larry Ellison, cofounder of Oracle Corp.

The inherent vice of capitalism is the uneven division of blessings, while the inherent virtue of socialism is the equal division of misery.

—Winston Churchill, former prime minister of the United Kingdom

---

I built them what they wanted and I made a profit off of it. Now they call me a god. . . . What fools these mortals be.

—Benjamin R. Smith, author (from his book *Atlas: A Novel*, 2012)

I had no ambition to make a fortune. Mere money making has never been my goal. I saw a marvelous future for our country, and I wanted to participate in the work of making our country great. I had an ambition to build.

—John D. Rockefeller, industrialist, cofounder of Standard Oil Co., and philanthropist

I also learned that I love making money. Anyone who is not afraid of work will be happy with the money they make.

—Gene Simmons, musician

Wealth is good when it brings joy to others.

—Og Mandino, author

I have always said that human beings are multidimensional beings. Their happiness comes from many sources, not, as our current economic framework assumes, just from making money.

—Muhammad Yunus, Nobel Peace Prize winner

———◆———

The greatest pleasure when I started making money was not buying cars or yachts but finding myself able to have as many freshly typed drafts as possible.

—Gore Vidal, writer and public intellectual

———◆———

The whole point of having money, and working and making money, is to enjoy and spend it.

—Irving Paul Lazar, talent agent

Making money is certainly the one addiction I cannot shake.

—Felix Dennis, publisher and poet

———◆———

You will find [money] the best of friends—if not the best friend—you have.

—John D. Rockefeller, industrialist, cofounder of Standard Oil Co., and philanthropist

———◆———

Take free money. No matter how in debt you are, if your employer offers a matching contribution on a 401(k) or other retirement vehicle, you must sign up and contribute enough to get the maximum company match each year. Think of it as a bonus.

—Suze Orman, personal finance expert

They're [the studios] definitely very serious about making money, and that's not a wrong thing, but you don't have to make money the same way all the time.

—Bill Murray, comedian and actor

My father said: "You must never try to make all the money that's in a deal. Let the other fellow make some money too, because if you have a reputation for always making all the money, you won't have many deals."

—J. Paul Getty, founder of Getty Oil Co.

Profits should be for a purpose. Profits should be productive. You should make money for producing benefits that make the world a better place. Making money is a good thing when it is made in service to humanity or the democracy.

—Andrew Young, US ambassador to the UN and Atlanta mayor

I'm not interested in making money. It's just that with my talent, I'm cursed with it.

—Noel Gallagher, English musician

The writer must earn money in order to be able to live and to write, but he must by no means live and write for the purpose of making money.

—Karl Marx, philosopher, economist, and revolutionary socialist

Human beings are much bigger than just making money.

—Muhammad Yunus, Nobel Peace Prize winner

The way to make money is to buy when blood is running in the streets.

—John D. Rockefeller, industrialist, cofounder of Standard Oil Co., and philanthropist

———◆———

Everyone knows that if you can keep on making money, everyone's happy.

—David Stern, commissioner of the National Basketball Association

———◆———

It's never been about making money.

—Rob Zombie, musician

The rich are always complaining.

—Zulu proverb

———◆———

Life started getting good when I started making money.

—Balthazar Getty, actor

———◆———

I don't believe in spending money lavishly, now that I'm making money.

—Ansel Elgort, actor and DJ

I love making money, but you can't live your life waiting to get rich in a job that no longer feeds you artistically.

—Julianna Margulies, actress

———◆———

My job is writing. I get paid to do it. When was the last time you heard someone challenge a doctor for making money off of cancer?

—Joyce Maynard, novelist and journalist

———◆———

Making money is not gonna change anything about what I am, except I won't answer the door.

—Abel Ferrara, filmmaker

Whether they run a record company or a grocery store, every boss will tell you you're in big trouble if you're borrowing more than you can ever afford to pay back. Delaying the pain for future generations is suicidal. We've got to start getting the deficit down right now, not next year.

—Simon Cowell, television producer

The worst crime against working people is a company which fails to operate at a profit.

—Samuel Gompers, labor union leader

The wealthiest Person on earth is one who is free from the love of Money.

—Andrew Darrah, author

It is no shame at all to work for money.
—African proverb

I cannot afford to waste my time making money.
—Louis Agassiz, author, doctor, scientist, and academic

Nothing wrong with making money or doing what you need to do to sell, but I think it shows when you're writing something to pay the bills and when you're writing something because it's really your version of the world.
—Laurell K. Hamilton, fantasy and romance writer

There is nothing wrong with making money, but it was just not in my family's habits to know how to do that. All we knew how to do was work, and we usually liked the work we did.

>—Stanley Hauerwas, theologian, ethicist, and public intellectual

———◆———

It isn't necessary to be rich and famous to be happy. It's only necessary to be rich.

>—Alan Alda, actor, director, and writer

———◆———

Making money is a hobby that will complement any other hobbies you have, beautifully.

>—Scott Alexander, author

The only point in making money is, you can tell some big shot where to go.

—Humphrey Bogart, actor

———◆———

Show me someone that doesn't pay attention to their money or is disrespectful of it and I will show you someone lacking money.

—Grant Cardone, motivational speaker and author

———◆———

The best way to boost the economy is to redistribute wealth downward, as poorer people tend to spend a higher proportion of their income.

—Ha-Joon Chang, South Korean economist

A business that makes nothing but money is a poor business.

—Henry Ford, founder of Ford Motor Co.

⎯⎯►◆◄⎯⎯

I'm not against the corporations. They are our wealth. But they are getting too greedy. I don't want to do away with corporations. I want them to make our cars, however, not our laws.

—Doris Haddock, political activist

⎯⎯►◆◄⎯⎯

I don't care half so much about making money as I do about making my point, and coming out ahead.

—Cornelius Vanderbilt, industrialist

The impression was gaining ground with me that it was a good thing to let the money be my slave and not make myself a slave to money.

> —John D. Rockefeller, industrialist, cofounder of Standard Oil Co., and philanthropist

You cannot be seeking yourself when you're making money.

> —Felix Dennis, publisher and poet

If you work just for money, you'll never make it, but if you love what you're doing and you always put the customer first, success will be yours.

> —Ray Kroc, chairman of McDonald's

The absolute fundamental aim is to make money out of satisfying customers.

—Sir John Egan, British industrialist

———◆———

[A]s far as I have heard or observed, the principal object is, not that mankind may be well and honestly clad, but, unquestionably, that corporations may be enriched.

—Henry David Thoreau, author, poet, philosopher, abolitionist, and naturalist

———◆———

It is a fact that around the world the elites of every country are making money.

—Hillary Clinton, US Secretary of State, US Senator, First Lady, and Presidential candidate

Getting money is like digging with a needle; spending it is like water soaking into sand.

  —Japanese proverb

Within the cult of Wall Street that forged Mitt Romney, making money justifies any behavior, no matter how venal.

  —Matt Taibbi, journalist

Business, you know, may bring money, but friendship hardly ever does.

  —Jane Austen, English novelist

I could have closed down bits of British Home Stores to make more money but it's not my style. I want to make my money as a retailer, not by putting people out of work.

—Philip Green, British businessman and the chairman of Arcadia Group

———◆———

My motivation has always been to do technology apps and companies, not making money. Just because the money's come, nothing's changed.

—Nick D'Aloisio, English computer programmer and Internet entrepreneur

———◆———

Making money is easy. It is. The difficult thing in life is not making it, it's keeping it.

—John McAfee, software entrepreneur

I always thought that I would spend the first half of my life making money so I can spend the second half of my life giving it all away. And one of the defining moments of my life was when I realized that I could do both at the same time with TOMS.

—Blake Mycoskie, founder of TOMS shoes, author, and philanthropist (from "Changing the World One Step at a Time," CNN.com, September 26, 2008)

The man who starts out simply with the idea of getting rich won't succeed; you must have a larger ambition.

—John D. Rockefeller, industrialist, cofounder of Standard Oil Co., and philanthropist

To do all the talking and not be willing to listen is a form of greed.

—Democritus, ancient Greek philosopher

[In 1910] War between nations is still a menace, but is as nothing in its destroying effects and results when compared with the civil war for individual wealth which has sprung into being throughout the world and made of every man a hypocrite and liar.

—King Gillette, founder of the Gillette Safety Razor Co.

Men are so simple, and governed so absolutely by their present needs, that he who wishes to deceive will never fail in finding willing dupes.

—Machiavelli, Italian Renaissance political philosopher

Today everything revolves around money and how much big fashion brands can pay an actress for a perfume deal or to wear a dress. Hollywood has become very superficial and not what I believe in.

—Giorgio Armani, fashion designer

Today, the concept of business is to make money. Making money is the name of the business.

—Muhammad Yunus, Nobel Peace Prize winner

❦

It is not the man who has little, but he who desires more, that is poor.

—Seneca, Roman Stoic philosopher, statesman, and
dramatist

❦

Major labels didn't start showing up really until they smelled money, and that's all they're ever going to be attracted to is money—that's the business they're in—making money.

—Ian MacKaye, singer, songwriter, and guitarist

Riches are not from abundance of worldly goods, but from a contented mind.

—Mohammed, Prophet of Islam

❦

It is wrong to assume that men of immense wealth are always happy.

—John D. Rockefeller, industrialist, cofounder of Standard Oil Co., and philanthropist

❦

Yet in buying goods it is best to pay ready money, because he that sells upon credit expects to lose five per cent, by bad debts; therefore, he charges on all he sells upon credit an advance that shall make up that deficiency.

—Benjamin Franklin, US founding father and inventor

Wealth is the abundance of something in such surplus that no conditions can destroy it. Making a lot of money is one thing, getting rich another. Creating wealth, well, that's what very few people ever learn. You have heard the expression "get rich quick," but you will never hear "get wealthy quick."

> —Grant Cardone, motivational speaker and author (from his article "8 Money Mistakes to Avoid on Your Way to Being Wealthy," *Entrepreneur*, August 11, 2014)

We reward people for making money off money, and moving money around and dividing up mortgages a thousand times over, selling it to China . . . and it becomes this shell game.

> —Michael Moore, filmmaker

I know of nothing more despicable and pathetic than a man who devotes all the hours of the waking day to the making of money for money's sake.

> —John D. Rockefeller, industrialist, cofounder of Standard Oil Co., and philanthropist

Misers make money their lord, but the spenders make it their slaves and servants.

—Michael Bassey Johnson, author

❦

Too many people miss the silver lining because they're expecting gold.

— Maurice Setter, English soccer player

❦

People who get trapped in the tunnel vision of making money think that is all there is to life.

—Felix Dennis, publisher and poet

A man's wealth must be determined by the relation of his desires and expenditures to his income. If he feels rich on ten dollars, and has everything else he desires, he really is rich.

—John D. Rockefeller, industrialist, cofounder of Standard Oil Co., and philanthropist

If you would like to know the value of money, try to borrow some.

—Benjamin Franklin, US founding father and inventor

If all you're doing is making money, you have a luxurious but empty life.

—Amanda Donohoe, actress

Determination and Focus

Determination and focus may be the most essential characteristics for a successful businessperson to have. Otherwise, he will be destined to abandon his goal, surrendering to the inevitable setbacks, frustration, and, ultimately, exhaustion common in climbing the corporate ladder or developing a business. Management and employees can hit loggerheads. Strategies go awry. Suppliers come up short. Business partners don't shoulder their load. Expect to encounter fierce rivals, fickle customers, and hesitant bankers. In short, be resolute. Muster the drive to stay the course.

It does not matter how slowly you go, so long as you do not stop.

—Confucius, Chinese philosopher

⬥

Success is not final, failure is not fatal: it is the courage to continue that counts.

—Winston Churchill, former prime minister of the United Kingdom

⬥

There are no traffic jams along the extra mile.

—Roger Staubach, professional quarterback

There is no substitute for hard work.
—Thomas Edison, inventor

—◆—

Genius is 1 percent inspiration and 99 percent perspiration. Accordingly a genius is often merely a talented person who has done all of his homework.
—Thomas Edison, inventor

—◆—

The one option in life that is almost always the wrong option is walking away and choosing not to be in the game.
—Bill Clinton, US president

The difference between ordinary and extraordinary is that little extra.

—Jimmy Johnson, professional football coach

I hated every minute of training, but I said, "Don't quit. Suffer now and live the rest of your life as a champion."

—Muhammad Ali, boxer and humanitarian

There's no luck in business. There's only drive, determination, and more drive.

—Sophie Kinsella, author (from her book *Shopaholic Takes Manhattan*, 2002)

Efforts and courage are not enough without purpose and direction.

—John F. Kennedy, US president

———◆———

Do not be discouraged . . . I had many refusals, I did not give up.

—John D. Rockefeller, industrialist, cofounder of Standard Oil Co., and philanthropist

———◆———

The only limit to your impact is your imagination and commitment.

—Anthony Robbins, motivational speaker, personal finance instructor, and self-help author

The majority of men meet with failure because of their lack of persistence in creating new plans to take the place of those which fail.

> —Napoleon Hill, pioneer of the modern genre of personal success (from his book *Think and Grow Rich*, 1937)

I think and think for months and years. Ninety-nine times, the conclusion is false. The hundredth time I am right.

> —Albert Einstein, developer of the theory of relativity

You have to serve many apprenticeships throughout your life. Show me somebody who won't serve an apprenticeship, and I'll show you somebody who won't go very far.

> —T. Boone Pickens, Texas oilman and investor (from his book *The Luckiest Guy in the World*, 2000)

Study, study and you will attain everything—wealth and fame. . . . You must know everything.

>—Isaac Babel, writer (from his story *"You Must Know Everything,"* 1966)

———◆———

Success usually comes to those who are too busy to be looking for it.

>—Henry David Thoreau, author, poet, philosopher, abolitionist, and naturalist

———◆———

If we attend continually and promptly to the little that we can do, we shall ere long be surprised to find how little remains that we cannot do.

>—Samuel Butler, novelist

Think and grow rich.

—Napoleon Hill, pioneer of the modern genre of personal success

❦

There are only two options regarding commitment. You're either in or out. There's no such thing as a life in-between.

—Pat Riley, professional basketball coach and executive

❦

Planning without action is futile, action without planning is fatal.

—Unknown

Don't fool yourself that important things can be put off till tomorrow; they can be put off forever, or not at all.
—Mignon McLaughlin, journalist and author

Far and away the best prize that life offers is the chance to work hard at work worth doing.
—Theodore Roosevelt, US president

We are not interested in the possibilities of defeat; they do not exist.
—Queen Victoria, English royalty

Never put off till tomorrow what you can do the day after tomorrow.

—Mark Twain, author and humorist

Great works are performed, not by strength, but by perseverance.

—Samuel Johnson, British author

Many of life's failures are people who did not realize how close they were to success when they gave up.

—Thomas Edison, inventor

I do not think that there is any other quality so essential to success of any kind as the quality of perseverance. It overcomes almost everything, even nature.

> —John D. Rockefeller, industrialist, cofounder of Standard Oil Co., and philanthropist

Winners lose more than losers. They win and lose more than losers because they stay in the game.

> —Terry Paulson, motivational speaker

If you're not gonna go all the way, why go at all?

> —Joe Namath, legendary professional quarterback

Work hard, have fun and make history.

—Jeff Bezos, founder of Amazon.com

———◆———

Success seems to be connected to action. Successful people keep moving. They make mistakes, but they don't quit.

—Conrad Hilton, founder of Hilton Hotels

———◆———

The difference between winning and losing is most often not quitting.

—Walt Disney, founder of Walt Disney Studios and theme parks

The biggest hurdle is rejection. Any business you start, be ready for it. The difference between successful people and unsuccessful people is the successful people do all the things the unsuccessful people don't want to do. When 10 doors are slammed in your face, go to door number 11 enthusiastically, with a smile on your face.

—John Paul DeJoria, businessman

Unless commitment is made, there are only promises and hopes . . . but no plans.

—Peter F. Drucker, management consultant, educator, and author

If you make the unconditional commitment to reach your most important goals, if the strength of your decision is sufficient, you will find the way and the power to achieve your goals.

—Robert Conklin, motivational writer

217

Effort only fully releases its reward after a person refuses to quit.

—Napoleon Hill, pioneer of the modern genre of personal success (from his book *Think and Grow Rich*, 1937)

———◆◆———

Giving up is the only sure way to fail.

—Gena Showalter, romance writer

———◆◆———

Nothing is so fatiguing as the eternal hanging on of an uncompleted task.

—William James, philosopher and psychologist

In the realm of ideas everything depends on enthusiasm . . . in the real world all rests on perseverance.

—Johann Wolfgang von Goethe, German writer and statesman

———◆———

Perseverance is not a long race; it is many short races one after another.

—Walter Elliott, priest (from his book *The Spiritual Life: Doctrine and Practice of Christian Perfection*, 2010)

———◆———

I am well known by my friends to be a workaholic—to their often justifiable annoyance. I am therefore keenly aware that such behavior is at best slightly pathological, and certainly in no sense makes one a better person.

—David Graeber, author, anthropologist, and anarchist activist

219

When you reach an obstacle, turn it into an opportunity. You have the choice. You can overcome and be a winner, or you can allow it to overcome you and be a loser. The choice is yours and yours alone. Refuse to throw in the towel. Go that extra mile that failures refuse to travel. It is far better to be exhausted from success than to be rested from failure.

—Mary Kay Ash, founder of Mary Kay Cosmetics

The best way to jumpstart a career is to say "yes" to every opportunity that comes along, whether it seems like it's way over your head or not worth doing. Then once you've said yes, no matter what the task is, do all the homework you possibly can to ensure you do a good job.

—Julia Boorstin, senior media and entertainment correspondent, CNBC

Theories can be wonderful—but the true genius is he who can sell two books where one was sold before.

—Nick Lyons, teacher, writer, and publisher

If you can't fly then run, if you can't run then walk, if you can't walk then crawl, but whatever you do you have to keep moving forward.

—Martin Luther King Jr., civil rights leader

If something is important enough, even if the odds are against you, you should still do it.

—Elon Musk, founder of Tesla Motors

The will to win, the desire to succeed, the urge to reach your full potential . . . These are the keys that will unlock the door to personal excellence.

—Confucius, Chinese philosopher

If you take someone who lacks the experience and the know-how but has the real desire and the willingness to work his tail off to get the job done, he'll make up for what he lacks. And that proved true nine times out of ten.

—Sam Walton, founder of Wal-Mart

Dreaming of being on Moon cannot get you there. It requires a focused and intelligent effort to achieve what you Dream.

—N. V. Sakhardande, author and management expert

Somehow I can't believe there aren't many heights that can't be scaled by one who knows the secret of making dreams come true. This special secret can be summarized in four C's. They are Curiosity, Confidence, Courage, and Constancy, and the greatest of these is Confidence.

—Walt Disney, founder of Walt Disney Studios and theme parks

I never did anything worth doing by accident, nor did any of my inventions come indirectly through accident, except the phonograph. No, when I have fully decided that a result is worth getting, I go about it, and make trial after trial, until it comes.

—Thomas Edison, inventor

———◆———

I've been absolutely terrified every moment of my life—and I've never let it keep me from doing a single thing I wanted to do.

—Georgia O'Keeffe, artist

———◆———

Persistence. It's that certain little spirit that compels you to continue just when you're at your most tired. It's that quality that forces you to persevere, find the route around the stone wall. It's the immovable stubbornness that will not allow you to cave in when everyone says give up.

—Estée Lauder, cofounder of Estée Lauder Companies

All of us have bad luck and good luck. The man who persists through the bad luck—who keeps right on going—is the man who is there when the good luck comes—and is ready to receive it.

—Robert Collier, self-help author

If you are going through hell, keep going.

—Winston Churchill, former prime minister of the United Kingdom

It's the constant and determined effort that breaks down all resistance and sweeps away all obstacles.

—Claude M. Bristol, author

You may make mistakes and get hurt, but you can't afford to wallow in self-pity. It's a lesson that's particularly important in business because you will undoubtedly get knocked down. That's when you have to determine not to be counted out, but get up and keep fighting.

—Gurbaksh Chahal, entrepreneur and author

Be courageous. I have seen many depressions in business. Always, America has emerged from these stronger and more prosperous. Be brave as your fathers before you. Have faith! Go forward.

—Thomas Edison, inventor

Strategy is all about commitment. If what you're doing isn't irrevocable, then you don't have a strategy—because anyone can do it. . . . I've always wanted to treat life like I was an invading army and there was no turning back.

—Troy Tyler, entrepreneur

Take up one idea. Make that one idea your life—think of it, dream of it, live on that idea. Let the brain, muscles, nerves, every part of your body, be full of that idea, and just leave every other idea alone. This is the way to success.

—Swami Vivekananda, Indian Hindu monk

Businesspeople are like sharks, not just because we're gray and slightly oily, or because our teeth trail the innards of those we have eviscerated, but because we must move forward or die.

—Stanley Bing, pen name of Gil Schwartz, business humorist and novelist

Effective performance is preceded by painstaking preparation.

—Brian Tracy, author

When I began my humanitarian work, I understood that in order to gain credibility I needed patience, commitment and unwavering perseverance. I needed to ignore the skeptics.

—Bianca Jagger, social and human rights advocate

———◆———

The harder you work, the harder it is to surrender.

—Vince Lombardi, professional football coaching legend

———◆———

All who have accomplished great things have had a great aim, have fixed their gaze on a goal which was high, one which sometimes seemed impossible.

—Orison Swett Marden, inspirational author and founder of *SUCCESS* magazine

The difference between a successful person and others is not a lack of strength, not a lack of knowledge, but rather a lack of will.

—Vince Lombardi, professional football coaching legend

You miss 100 percent of the shots you don't take.

—Wayne Gretzky, hockey great

Forget past mistakes. Forget failures. Forget everything except what you're going to do now and do it.

—William Durant, cofounder of General Motors

Let me tell you the secret that has led me to my goal: my strength lies solely in my tenacity.

—Louis Pasteur, chemist and investor of pasteurization

———◆———

I quickly learned that if I kept at it and plowed right through the rejections I would eventually get somebody to buy my wares.

—Charles R. Schwab, founder of Charles Schwab Corp.

———◆———

Fidelity is seven-tenths of business success.

—James Parton, author

Do not many of us who fail to achieve big things . . . fail because we lack concentration—the art of concentrating the mind on the thing to be done at the proper time and to the exclusion of everything else?

> —John D. Rockefeller, industrialist, cofounder of Standard Oil Co., and philanthropist

Men in general judge more by appearances than by reality. All men have eyes, but few have the gift of penetration.

> —Machiavelli, Italian Renaissance political philosopher

If you spend your life trying to be good at everything, you will never be great at anything.

> —Tom Rath, author

If you take an idea and just hold it in your head, you unconsciously start to do things that advance you toward that goal.

—Biz Stone, cofounder of Twitter

Any idea, plan, or purpose may be placed in the mind through repetition of thought.

—Napoleon Hill, pioneer of the modern genre of personal success

To be disciplined is to follow in a good way. To be self disciplined is to follow in a better way.

—Corita Kent, Catholic nun, artist, and educator

Perpetual devotion to what a man calls his business is only to be sustained by perpetual neglect of many other things.

——Robert Louis Stevenson, Scottish poet and novelist

Whatever you are by nature, keep to it; never desert your line of talent. Be what nature intended you for and you will succeed.

——Sydney Smith, English essayist

Concentrate all your thoughts upon the work in hand. The Sun's rays do not burn until brought to a focus.

——Alexander Graham Bell, chief inventor of the telephone

Not being aware of all you have to do is much like having a credit card for which you don't know the balance or the limit—it's a lot easier to be irresponsible.

    —David Allen, author

I studied the lives of great men and famous women, and I found that the men and women who got to the top were those who did the jobs they had in hand, with everything they had of energy and enthusiasm and hard work.

    —Harry Truman, US president

Think of many things; do one.

    —Portuguese proverb

A dream doesn't become reality through magic; it takes sweat, determination and hard work.

— Colin Powell, US Secretary of State and Chairman of the Joint Chiefs of Staff

Without purpose ... goals, ambitions, and dreams aren't worth the paper they're written on. Without direction, a business plan, no matter how carefully written, is simply a bunch of words ruining a perfectly good blank sheet of paper.

— Peter J. Patsula, author and founder of Patsula Media (from his online publication *The Entrepreneur's Guidebook Series*, 2001–2007)

I never dreamed about success. I worked for it.

— Estée Lauder, cofounder of Estée Lauder Companies

When your mind is clear, action is focused.
  —Lisa A. Mininni, author

———◆———

Most of the important things in the world have been accomplished by people who have kept on trying when there seemed to be no hope at all.
  —Dale Carnegie, writer, lecturer, and developer of self-improvement courses

———◆———

Look well to this day. Yesterday is but a dream and tomorrow is only a vision. But today well lived makes every yesterday a dream of happiness and every tomorrow a vision of hope. Look well therefore to this day.
  —Francis Gray, Massachusetts politician

Singleness of purpose is one of the chief essentials for success in life, no matter what may be one's aim.
—John D. Rockefeller, industrialist, cofounder of Standard Oil Co., and philanthropist

---

Focus is so critically important. . . . Saying "no" to great ideas is necessary to get to the brilliant ones. At every step of the way you have to cut towards one path. It's such a hard thing to do as an entrepreneur because you don't really have the confidence in where you're going yourself.
—Dane Atkinson, CEO of SumAll

I've always believed that if you stick to a thought and carefully avoid distraction along the way, you can fulfill a dream. My whole life has been about fulfilling dreams. I kept my eye on the target, whatever that target was. Whether your target is big or small, grand or simple, ambitious or personal, I've always believed that success comes from not letting your eyes stray from that target. Anyone who wants to achieve a dream must stay strong, focused and steady.
—Estée Lauder, cofounder of Estée Lauder Companies

Failure, Fear, and Adversity

The failure rate of businesses is notoriously high—as steep as nine of every ten start-ups, by some accounts. Even the 10 percent or so that survive become acquainted with failure. Hired after careful vetting, a new employee flames out. Highly promoted merchandise languishes on store shelves. A lawsuit against a rival is decided in the opponent's favor. And, to be sure, the most successful businesses can count on experiencing adversity as well. Quarterly profits drop. An ascendant rival appears on the horizon. A visionary faces unanimous skepticism. Given the realities of business life, successful people in the business world have adopted a universal coping mechanism: they subscribe to the idea that setbacks are strengthening. Hardships test their mettle. Failures set the stage for a rebound. Redemption is just around the corner. Although it may seem perverse, applaud failure.

Don't be afraid of failure; be afraid of petty success.

—Maud Adams, actress

———◆———

There is no failure, only feedback.

—Robert G. Allen, author

———◆———

You may encounter many defeats, but you must not be defeated. In fact, it may be necessary to encounter the defeats, so you can know who you are, what you can rise from, how you can still come out of it.

—Maya Angelou, author and poet

Whatever failures I have known, whatever errors I have committed, whatever follies I have witnessed in private and public life have been the consequence of action without thought.

> —Bernard Baruch, financier, stock investor, philanthropist, and statesman

Yesterday's failures are today's seeds that must be diligently planted to be able to abundantly harvest tomorrow's success.

> —Anonymous

Would you like me to give you a formula for success? It's quite simple, really. Double your rate of failure. You are thinking of failure as the enemy of success. But it isn't at all. You can be discouraged by failure or you can learn from it. So go ahead and make mistakes. Make all you can. Because remember, that's where you'll find success.

> —Thomas J. Watson, chairman and CEO of IBM

Every failure, obstacle or hardship is an opportunity in disguise. Success in many cases is failure turned inside out. The greatest pollution problem we face today is negativity. Eliminate the negative attitude and believe you can do anything. Replace if I can, I hope, and maybe with can, I will, and I must.

—Mary Kay Ash, founder of Mary Kay Cosmetics

A man so busy cannot be always right. We are all bound to make mistakes at times.

—John D. Rockefeller, industrialist, cofounder of Standard Oil Co., and philanthropist

We are all failures—at least the best of us are.

—J. M. Barrie, Scottish novelist and playwright

Failure is the new black.

—Jonathan Becher, chief digital officer of SAP

Go on failing. Go on. Only next time, try to fail better.

—Samuel Beckett, novelist, playwright, theatre director, and poet

---

All my successes have been built on my failures.

—Benjamin Disraeli, British prime minister and writer

We never claim that our approach is the right one—just that it's ours—and over the last two decades, we've collected a large group of like-minded people. . . . One area where I think we are especially distinctive is failure. I believe we are the best place in the world to fail (we have plenty of practice!), and failure and invention are inseparable twins.

—Jeff Bezos, founder of Amazon.com

Don't fear failure so much that you refuse to try new things.

—Louis Boone, author

None of us can be free of conflict and woe. Even the greatest men have to accept disappointments as their daily bread. . . . The art of living lies less in eliminating our troubles than in growing with them.

—Bernard Baruch, financier, stock investor, philanthropist, and statesman

A failure establishes only this: that our determination to succeed was not strong enough.

— Christian Nestell Bovee, writer

———◆———

Failure is the condiment that gives success its flavor.

—Truman Capote, novelist, screenwriter, playwright, and actor

———◆———

Develop success from failures. Discouragement and failure are two of the surest stepping stones to success.

—Dale Carnegie, writer, lecturer, and the developer self-improvement courses

For every failure, there's an alternative course of action. You just have to find it. When you come to a road block, take a detour.

—Mary Kay Ash, founder of Mary Kay Cosmetics

You build on failure. You use it as a stepping stone. Close the door on the past. You don't try to forget the mistakes, but you don't dwell on it. You don't let it have any of your energy, or any of your time, or any of your space.

—Johnny Cash, country singer

Success is often achieved by those who don't know that failure is inevitable.

—Coco Chanel, fashion designer

Nobody's going to win all the time. On the highway of life you can't always be in the fast lane.

—Haruki Murakami, Japanese writer

Think like a queen. A queen is not afraid to fail. Failure is another stepping stone to greatness.

—Oprah Winfrey, media mogul, television host, and actress

Show me a failure, and I will show you a man who does today what he should have done yesterday.

—Ajaero Tony Martins, Nigerian entrepreneur and investor

Success is walking from failure to failure with no loss of enthusiasm.

—Winston Churchill, former prime minister of the United Kingdom

——◆◆◆◆——

If you live long enough, you'll make mistakes. But if you learn from them, you'll be a better person.

—Bill Clinton, US president

——◆◆◆◆——

It was my fear of failure that first kept me from attempting the master work. Now, I'm beginning what I could have started ten years ago. But I'm happy at least that I didn't wait twenty years.

—Paulo Coelho, Brazilian lyricist and novelist

Greatness is not achieved by never falling but by rising each time we fall.

—Confucius, Chinese philosopher

—◆—

Mistakes are part of the game. It's how well you recover from them, that's the mark of a great player.

—Alice Cooper, rock musician

—◆—

It's failure that gives you the proper perspective on success.

—Ellen DeGeneres, talk show host and actress

Be the one thing you think you cannot do. Fail at it. Try again. Do better the second time. The only people who never tumble are those who never mount the high wire. This is your moment, own it.

> —Oprah Winfrey, media mogul, television host, and actress

Success, after all, loves a witness, but failure can't exist without one.

> —Junot Diaz, writer and creative writing professor

All my successes have been built on my failures.

> —Benjamin Disraeli, British prime minister and writer

Life is all about learning and one of the most memorable ways of learning something is by messing up.

> —Dr. Wayne W. Dyer, philosopher, self-help author, and motivational speaker

It is on our failures that we base a new and different and better success.

> —Havelock Ellis, English physician, writer, intellectual, and social reformer

The greatest barrier to success is the fear of failure.

> —Sven-Göran Eriksson, Swedish football manager and former player

He who looks into the future with the eyes of fear will see nothing but failure.

—Dr. O. Ezekiel, minister

———◆———

There are no mistakes, only opportunities.

—Tina Fey, actress and comedian

———◆———

The important thing is not being afraid to take a chance. Remember, the greatest failure is to not try. Once you find something you love to do, be the best at doing it.

—Debbi Fields, founder of Mrs. Fields Bakeries

The phoenix must burn to emerge.

 —Janet Fitch, author

The only real mistake is the one from which we learn nothing.

 —Henry Ford, founder of Ford Motor Co.

How many people are completely successful in every department of life? Not one. The most successful people are the ones who learn from their mistakes and turn their failures into opportunities.

 —Zig Ziglar, author and motivational speaker

251

Reward worthy failure–Experimentation.

— Bill Gates, cofounder of Microsoft and
philanthropist

No human ever became interesting by not failing. The
more you fail and recover and improve, the better you
are as a person. Ever meet someone who's always had
everything work out for them with zero struggle? They
usually have the depth of a puddle. Or they don't exist.

— Chris Hardwick, television host, stand-up comedian,
actor, and writer

Planning is an unnatural process; it is much more fun
to do something. The nicest thing about not planning
is that failure comes as a complete surprise, rather than
being preceded by a period of worry and depression.

— Sir John Harvey-Jones, English businessman

Notice the difference between what happens when a man says to himself, "I have failed three times," and what happens when he says, "I am a failure."

—S. I. Hayakawa, US senator

———◆———

Every adversity, every failure, every heartache carries with it the seed of an equal or greater benefit.

—Napoleon Hill, pioneer of the modern genre of personal success

———◆———

Failure can either be a stepping stone to success or a stumbling stone to defeat.

—Ron Holland, author (from his book *Talk & Grow Rich: How to Create Wealth Without Capital,* 1900)

Don't worry about failure; you only have to be right once.

—Drew Houston, founder and CEO of Dropbox

◆—◆◆—◆

A failure is a man who has blundered, but is not able to cash in the experience.

—Elbert Hubbard, writer, publisher, artist, and philosopher

◆—◆◆—◆

Surviving a failure gives you more self-confidence. Failures are great learning tools . . . but they must be kept to a minimum.

—Jeffrey Immelt, chairman and CEO of GE

I've missed more than 9,000 shots in my career. I've lost almost 300 games. 26 times I've been trusted to take the game winning shot and missed. I've failed over and over and over again in my life, and that is why I succeed.
—Michael Jordan, NBA legend

There is only one thing that makes a dream impossible to achieve: the fear of failure.
—Paulo Coelho, Brazilian lyricist and novelist

If you are not failing, you are not growing.
—H. Stanley Judd, author

If people are failing, they look inept. If people are succeeding, they look strong and good and competent. That's the "halo effect." Your first impression of a thing sets up your subsequent beliefs. If the company looks inept to you, you may assume everything else they do is inept.

—Daniel Kahneman, psychologist and winner of the Nobel Memorial Prize in Economic Sciences

Only those who dare to fail greatly can ever achieve greatly.

—Robert F. Kennedy, US senator and US attorney general

Winners are not afraid of losing. But losers are. Failure is part of the process of success. People who avoid failure also avoid success.

—Robert Kiyosaki, investor, self-help author, and motivational speaker

Failures are finger posts on the road to achievement.
—C. S. Lewis, British novelist, poet, literary critic,
essayist, broadcaster, and lecturer

———✦———

Failure is not a resting place. It is an opportunity to begin again more intelligently.
—Henry Ford, founder of Ford Motor Co.

———✦———

While one person hesitates because he feels inferior, the other is busy making mistakes and becoming superior.
—Henry C. Link, employment psychologist

My first six years in the business were hopeless. There are a lot of times when you sit and you say "Why am I doing this? I'll never make it. It's just not going to happen. I should go out and get a real job, and try to survive."

—George Lucas, creator of *Star Wars* and *Indiana Jones*

The business empires built by successful entrepreneurs were erected on the foundation of past failures.

—Ajaero Tony Martins, Nigerian entrepreneur and investor

It is better to fail in originality than to succeed in imitation.

—Herman Melville, novelist and poet

I believe in trusting men, not only once but twice—in giving a failure another chance.

—J. C. Penney, founder of retail chain JCPenney

———◆———

Failures are like skinned knees, painful but superficial.

—Ross Perot, businessman and Reform Party presidential candidate

———◆———

There are two kinds of failures: those who thought and never did, and those who did and never thought.

—Laurence J. Peter, author

If you have made mistakes, there is always another chance for you. You may have a fresh start any moment you choose, for this thing we call "failure" is not the falling down, but the staying down.

—Mary Pickford, actress, writer, director, and producer

In other words, don't expect to always be great. Disappointments, failures and setbacks are a normal part of the lifecycle of a unit or a company and what the leader has to do is constantly be up and say, "We have a problem, let's go and get it."

—Colin Powell, US Secretary of State and Chairman of the Joint Chiefs of Staff

I can accept failure; everyone fails at something. But I cannot accept not trying.

—Michael Jordan, NBA legend

To avoid failure is to limit accomplishment.

> —Will Rogers, American cowboy, vaudeville performer, humorist, newspaper columnist, social commentator, and stage and motion picture actor

You always pass failure on your way to success.

> —Mickey Rooney, actor and comedian

Don't be afraid to give up the good to go for the great.

> —John D. Rockefeller, industrialist, cofounder of Standard Oil Co., and philanthropist

The way I see it, if you want the rainbow, you gotta put up with the rain.

—Dolly Parton, country singer

It is hard to fail, but it is worse never to have tried to succeed.

—Theodore Roosevelt, US president

Failure is so important. We speak about success all the time. It is the ability to resist failure or use failure that often leads to greater success. I've met people who don't want to try for fear of failing.

—J. K. Rowling, *Harry Potter* author

I like to fail. I have had so many failures and each time I have failed, I have figured out how to grow.

—Michael Rubin, e-commerce entrepreneur

When I was a young man I observed that nine out of ten things I did were failures. I didn't want to be a failure, so I did ten times more work.

—George Bernard Shaw, Irish playwright, critic, and polemicist

Failure is the opportunity to begin again, more intelligently.

—Henry Ford, founder of Ford Motor Co.

Losers quit when they fail. Winners fail until they succeed.

—Robert Kiyosaki, investor, self-help author, and motivational speaker

Like success, failure is many things to many people. With Positive Mental Attitude, failure is a learning experience, a rung on the ladder, and a plateau at which to get your thoughts in order to prepare to try again.

—W. Clement Stone, businessman, philanthropist, and self-help author

More men fail through lack of purpose than lack of talent.

—Billy Sunday, baseball professional turned evangelist

Sheer persistence is the difference between success and failure.

> —Donald Trump, real estate developer, author, and Presidential candidate

———•———

Rejection is one step to get you closer to the destination if you simply stay persistent!

> —Sarah Tse, artist

———•———

Many people fail in life, not for lack of ability or brains or even courage but simply because they have never organized their energies around a goal.

> —Elbert Hubbard, writer, publisher, artist, and philosopher

Remember the two benefits of failure. First, if you do fail, you learn what doesn't work; and second, the failure gives you the opportunity to try a new approach.

—Roger Von Oech, speaker, author, and toy maker

———

Failure should be our teacher, not our undertaker. Failure is delay, not defeat. It is a temporary detour, not a dead end. Failure is something we can avoid only by saying nothing, doing nothing, and being nothing.

—Denis Waitley, motivational speaker, writer, and consultant

———

Success has many fathers but failure is an orphan.

—John F. Kennedy, US president

I've learned that mistakes can often be as good a teacher as success.

  —Jack Welch, chairman and CEO of GE

What seems to us as bitter trials are often blessings in disguise.

  —Oscar Wilde, Irish playwright, novelist, essayist, and poet

---

I don't believe in failure. It's not failure if you enjoyed the process.

  —Oprah Winfrey, media mogul, television host, and actress

In this business, by the time you realize you're in trouble, it's too late to save yourself. Unless you're running scared all the time, you're gone.

—Bill Gates, cofounder of Microsoft and philanthropist

It's common sense to take a method and try it. If it fails, admit it frankly and try another. But above all, try something.

—Franklin D. Roosevelt, US president

Defeat is not the worst of failures. Not to have tried is the true failure.

—George Edward Woodberry, literary critic and poet

Take a risk to start a new business even if you are still working part-time.

—Emenike Emmanuel, Nigerian soccer player

Failure isn't fatal, but failure to change might be.

—John Wooden, legendary UCLA basketball coach

If you don't try at anything, you can't fail. . . . It takes backbone to lead the life you want.

—Richard Yates, fiction writer

It's not how far you fall, but how high you bounce that counts.

—Zig Ziglar, author and motivational speaker

Everyone is your best friend when you are successful. Make sure that the people that you surround yourself with are also the people that you are not afraid of failing with.

—Paula Abdul, singer-songwriter

Edison failed 10,000 times before he made the electric light. Do not be discouraged if you fail a few times.

—Napoleon Hill, pioneer of the modern genre of personal success

I have heard many men talk intelligently, even brilliantly about something—only to see them proven powerless when it comes to acting on what they believe.

—Bernard Baruch, financier, stock investor, philanthropist, and statesman

———◆———

I didn't think I'd regret trying and failing. . . . I suspected I would always be haunted by a decision to not try at all.

—Jeff Bezos, founder of Amazon.com

———◆———

It's very important to take risks. I think that research is very important, but in the end you have to work from your instinct and feeling and take those risks and be fearless. When I hear a company is being run by a team, my heart sinks, because you need to have that leader with a vision and heart that can move things forward.

—Anna Wintour, *Vogue* magazine editor

There are no rules. You don't learn to walk by following rules. You learn by doing, and by falling over, and it's because you fall over that you learn to save yourself from falling over.

 —Sir Richard Branson, billionaire entrepreneur
  and founder of Virgin Airlines

The winners in life think constantly in terms of I can, I will, and I am. Losers, on the other hand, concentrate their waking thoughts on what they should have or would have done, or what they can't do.

 —Denis Waitley, motivational speaker, writer, and
  consultant

Failing conventionally is the route to go; as a group, lemmings may have a rotten image, but no individual lemming has ever received bad press.

 —Warren Buffett, legendary investor and chairman of
  Berkshire Hathaway

You can't have any successes unless you can accept failure.

> —George Cukor, film director

———◆———

Success is a poor teacher. We learn the most about ourselves when we fail, so don't be afraid of failing. Failing is part of the process of success. You cannot have success without failure.

> — Robert T. Kiyosaki, author

———◆———

Sometimes by losing a battle, you will find a new way to win the war.

> —Donald Trump, real estate developer, author, and presidential candidate

When we give ourselves permission to fail, we, at the same time, give ourselves permission to excel.

—Eloise Ristad, author

Don't argue for other people's weaknesses. Don't argue for your own. When you make a mistake, admit it, correct it, and learn from it, immediately.

—Stephen Covey, educator, author, and businessman

Restlessness is discontent and discontent is the first necessity of progress. Show me a thoroughly satisfied man and I will show you a failure.

—Thomas Edison, inventor

To avoid criticism, do nothing, say nothing, be nothing.
—Elbert Hubbard, writer, publisher, artist, and
philosopher

———◆———

Victory goes to the player who makes the next-to-last mistake.
—Savielly Tartakower, Polish and French chess
grandmaster

———◆———

A champion is afraid of losing. Everyone else is afraid of winning.
—Billie Jean King, world champion tennis player

275

Nobody likes to fail. I want to succeed in everything I do, which isn't much. But the things that I'm really passionate about, if I fail at those, if I'm not successful, what do I have?

  —Eminem, rapper

The successful man will profit from his mistakes and try again in a different way.

  —Dale Carnegie, writer, lecturer, and developer of self-improvement courses

Our business in this world is not to succeed, but to continue to fail in good spirits.

  —Robert Louis Stevenson, Scottish poet and novelist

For maximum attention, nothing beats a good mistake.
—Unknown

———◆———

If you're not making mistakes, you're not taking risks, and that means you're not going anywhere. The key is to make mistakes faster than the competition, so you have more chances to learn and win.
—John W. Holt, author

———◆———

You always learn a lot more when you lose than when you win.
—African proverb

Rejection is an opportunity for your selection.
—Bernard Branson, author

———◈———

You cannot expect to create a machine, ever, that will merely turn out hundred-dollar bills without problems.
—Nick Lyons, teacher, writer, and publisher

———◈———

Before success comes in any man's life, he's sure to meet with much temporary defeat and, perhaps, some failures. When defeat overtakes a man, the easiest and the most logical thing to do is to quit. That's exactly what the majority of men do.
—Napoleon Hill, pioneer of the modern genre of personal success (from his book *Think and Grow Rich*, 1937)

You can look at the situation and feel victimized. Or you can look at it and be excited about conquering the challenges and opportunities it presents.

—Jack Welch, chairman and CEO of GE (from his book *Winning: The Ultimate Business How-To Book*, 2005)

I have had all the disadvantages required for success.

—Larry Ellison, cofounder of Oracle Corp. (from *60 Minutes* interview on CBS, February 23, 2004)

If there is no struggle, there is no progress.

—Frederick Douglass, African-American abolitionist, orator, and writer (from his "West India Emancipation" speech on August 3, 1857)

To escape fear, you have to go through it, not around.

—Richie Norton, author (from his book *Résumés Are Dead and What to Do About It*, 2012)

———◆———

Sometimes adversity is what you need to face in order to become successful.

—Zig Ziglar, author and motivational speaker

———◆———

The weather isn't always balmy. Nor would one want it so.

—Nick Lyons, teacher, writer, and publisher

Creativity, Innovation, and Risk

People of a certain age long to discover the mythical fountain of youth. In a similar vein, businesspeople want to crack the code on how to isolate and then implant the creativity gene within the corporate workforce. In the current business zeitgeist of high-velocity, technology-fueled change, corporate leaders live in constant dread of falling behind. Their nightmare scenario: becoming yesterday's discard in the wake of an ascendant rival's sudden appearance on the horizon with the next shiny new thing. They become obsessed with fostering a corporate culture of perpetual creativity. "Thinking outside the box" is a mantra, as is risk. And the topic of "innovation" is a mainstay of business media. Ideas can often be the difference between stagnation and success.

Innovation is the specific instrument of entrepreneurship . . . the act that endows resources with a new capacity to create wealth.

> —Peter F. Drucker, management consultant, educator, and author (from his book *Innovation and Entrepreneurship,* 1985)

The heart and soul of the company is creativity and innovation.

> —Bob Iger, chairman and CEO, Walt Disney Co.

Imagination is everything. It is the preview of life's coming attractions.

> —Albert Einstein, developer of the theory of relativity

Business has only two functions—marketing and innovation.

—Milan Kundera, novelist

——◆——

Sometimes when you innovate, you make mistakes. It is best to admit them quickly and get on with improving your other innovations.

—Steve Jobs, cofounder of Apple and Pixar Animation (from the *Wall Street Journal,* May 25, 1993)

——◆——

The only purpose of a business is to bring in a customer; and there are really only two ways to do it—through marketing or innovation.

—Noel Peebles, businessman and author

Most of us understand that innovation is enormously important. It's the only insurance against irrelevance. It's the only guarantee of long-term customer loyalty. It's the only strategy for out-performing a dismal economy.

—Gary Hamel, management expert (from "Gary Hamel on Innovating Innovation," *Forbes,* December 4, 2012)

Think outside of your experience, or your disciplines. The most interesting ideas come from the confluence, the intersections of disciplines. This is why people with an artistic background who go into business succeed. They really do bring something unique. The more boxes and points of context you have between them, the better the ideas will be. We are drowning in information, and very little knowledge.

—Fareed Zakaria, CNN host and *New York Times* best-selling author

There is no evidence for what has not been created yet; only insight, purpose, passion and a willingness to move into what could be instead of what is. . . . Truly innovative companies are not afraid to let go and create the next market shift.

—Christine Day, CEO of Luvo (from "The Best Business Advice You'll Ever Get," *Entrepreneur,* July 2, 2014)

◆

All of these [concepts] started as me working in my apartment building on something I thought would be cool. . . . All are projects that turned into products that turned into companies.

—Dennis Crowley, CEO of Foursquare (from "The Best Business Advice You'll Ever Get," *Entrepreneur,* July 2, 2014)

A lot of what is wrong with corporate America has to do with a culture filled with antibodies trained to expel anything different. HR departments often want cookie cutter employees, which inevitably results in cookie cutter solutions.

—Nolan Bushnell, engineer and entrepreneur (from "How Not to Turn Away the Next Steve Jobs," *Inc.,* April 2, 2013)

When you innovate, you've got to be prepared for everyone telling you you're nuts.

—Larry Ellison, cofounder of Oracle Corp.

Invention is not enough. Tesla invented the electric power we use, but he struggled to get it out to people. You have to combine both things: invention and innovation focus, plus the company that can commercialize things and get them to people.

—Larry Page, cofounder of Google

Just build things and find out if they work.

—Ben Silbermann, founder of Pinterest

Be fearless. Have the courage to take risks. Go where there are no guarantees. Get out of your comfort zone even if it means being uncomfortable. The road less traveled is sometimes fraught with barricades, bumps, and uncharted terrain. But it is on that road where your character is truly tested. Have the courage to accept that you're not perfect, nothing is and no one is—and that's OK.

—Katie Couric, television and Yahoo! News anchor

Once we accept our limits, we go beyond them.

—Albert Einstein, developer of the theory of relativity

A great entrepreneur can take a bad idea and turn it into something incredible. . . .

—Peter Relan, entrepreneur

———⬥———

If you give people tools, and they use their natural abilities and their curiosity, they will develop things in ways that will surprise you very much beyond what you might have expected.

—Bill Gates, cofounder of Microsoft and philanthropist

———⬥———

Your personal life, your professional life, and your creative life are all intertwined. I went through a few very difficult years where I felt like a failure. But it was actually really important for me to go through that. Struggle, for me, is the most inspirational thing in the world at the end of the day—as long as you treat it that way.

—Skylar Grey, singer and songwriter

Over the years, I have learned that every significant invention has several characteristics. By definition it must be startling, unexpected, and must come into a world that is not prepared for it. If the world were prepared for it, it would not be much of an invention.

> —Dr. Edwin Land, cofounder of the Polaroid Corp. (from *Forbes* magazine, April 1, 1975)

To discover better ways of doing things one must question existent methods and practices and be courageous enough to gamble on something new or something different.

> —Clarence Birdseye, inventor, entrepreneur, and pioneer of the frozen foods industry (from *The American* magazine, vol. 151, 1951)

Taking chances almost always makes for happy endings.

> —Barbara Corcoran, businesswoman, investor, syndicated columnist, author, and television personality

The power to take risks is the adrenalin of all business enterprises—but betting the farm frequently—or even ever is for gamblers, not businessmen.

—Nick Lyons, teacher, writer, and publisher

The important thing is not being afraid to take a chance. Remember, the greatest failure is to not try. Once you find something you love to do, be the best at doing it.

—Debbi Fields, founder of Mrs. Fields Bakeries

Don't let the fear of losing be greater than the excitement of winning.

—Robert Kiyosaki, entrepreneur and author

Any youth who makes security his main goal shackles himself at the very start of life's race. He will go much farther, in all probability, if he steps out for himself, asks questions, and takes chances.

—Clarence Birdseye, inventor, entrepreneur, and pioneer of the frozen foods industry

———◆———

In a world that's changing really quickly, the only strategy that is guaranteed to fail is not taking risks.

—Mark Zuckerberg, cofounder and CEO of Facebook

———◆———

Women don't take enough risks. Men are just "foot on the gas pedal." We're not going to close the achievement gap until we close the ambition gap.

—Sheryl Sandberg, chief operating officer of Facebook

I always did something I was a little not ready to do. I think that's how you grow. When there's that moment of "Wow, I'm not really sure I can do this," and you push through those moments, that's when you have a breakthrough.

—Marissa Mayer, CEO of Yahoo

———

I insist on a lot of time being spent, almost every day, to just sit and think. That is very uncommon in American business. I read and think. So I do more reading and thinking, and make less impulse decisions than most people in business. I do it because I like this kind of life.

—Warren Buffett, legendary investor and CEO of Berkshire Hathaway

———

We all sort of do want incentives for creative people to still exist at a certain level. You know, maybe rock stars shouldn't make as much; who knows? But you want as much creativity to take place in the future as took place in the past.

—Bill Gates, cofounder of Microsoft and philanthropist

We don't grow unless we take risks. Any successful company is riddled with failures.

—James E. Burke, CEO of Johnson & Johnson

———◆———

When you take risks you learn that there will be times when you succeed and there will be times when you fail, and both are equally important.

—Ellen DeGeneres, talk show host and actress

———◆———

If you're not prepared to be wrong, you'll never come up with anything original.

—Ken Robinson, English author and international advisor on art education

The price of inaction is far greater than the cost of a mistake.

—Meg Whitman, CEO of Hewlett Packard

To win without risk is to triumph without glory.

—Pierre Corneille, French dramatist

Unless you're willing to have a go, fail miserably, and have another go, success won't happen.

—Phillip Adams, film producer, broadcaster, and writer

The biggest risk is not taking any risk. . . . In a world that's changing really quickly, the only strategy that is guaranteed to fail is not taking risks.

—Mark Zuckerberg, cofounder and CEO of Facebook

———<>———

Life isn't worth living unless you're willing to take some big chances and go for broke.

—Eliot Wigginton, oral historian, folklorist, writer, and educator

———<>———

Security is mostly a superstition. It does not exist in nature, nor do the children of men as a whole experience it. Avoiding danger is no safer in the long run than outright exposure. Life is either a daring adventure, or nothing.

—Helen Keller, journalist, author, and activist for the blind

You overestimate the risk in your mind. . . . You see yourself as more vulnerable, and you forget how capable and competent you are.

—Marci G. Fox, psychologist

Every day, you'll have opportunities to take chances and to work outside your safety net. Sure, it's a lot easier to stay in your comfort zone . . . in my case, business suits and real estate . . . but sometimes you have to take risks. When the risks pay off, that's when you reap the biggest rewards.

—Donald Trump, real estate developer, author, and presidential candidate

Every business and every product has risks. You can't get around it.

—Lee Iacocca, chairman and CEO of Chrysler Motors

In business the man who engages in the most adventures is surest to come out unhurt.

    —Karl Marx, philosopher, economist, and revolutionary socialist

———◆———

Customers are willing to try new things, and if you can survive, you will have fewer competitors. It's like entering the eye of the storm. As long as you are strong enough to survive, you can end up in still water by yourself.

    —Brian Chesky, cofounder and CEO of Airbnb

———◆———

If you're not failing every now and again, it's a sign you're not doing anything very innovative.

    —Woody Allen, actor and filmmaker

Creativity is key to productivity and prosperity.

    —Ifeanyi Enoch Onuoha, author, inspirational speaker, and life coach

In order to be irreplaceable one must always be different.

    —Coco Chanel, fashion designer

Always think outside the box and embrace opportunities that appear, wherever they might be.

    —Lakshmi Mittal, Indian steel magnate

For every dilemma, find at least three or four possible solutions. The creative process leads to better results.

—Marilyn Suttle, author and motivational speaker

The ability to listen, watch and draw lessons from obvious and unlikely places breeds originality and growth.

—Biz Stone, cofounder of Twitter

He who can no longer pause to wonder and stand rapt in awe is as good as dead; his eyes are closed.

—Albert Einstein, developer of the theory of relativity

I have not failed. I've just found 10,000 ways that won't work.

—Thomas Edison, inventor

⋲•⋺

The simple joy of taking an idea into one's own hands and giving it proper form, that's exciting.

—George Nelson, industrial designer and a founder of American Modernism

⋲•⋺

We are always saying to ourselves, we have to innovate. We've got to come up with that breakthrough. In fact, the way software works, so long as you are using your existing software, you don't pay us anything at all. So we're only paid for breakthroughs.

—Bill Gates, cofounder of Microsoft and philanthropist

Imagination is more important than knowledge.

—Albert Einstein, developer of the theory of relativity

———◆———

To know is nothing at all; to imagine is everything.

—Anatole France, poet and journalist

———◆———

Testing assumptions allows you the power to create possibilities.

—Lisa A. Mininni, author

It is the supreme art of the teacher to awaken joy in creative expression and knowledge.

—Albert Einstein, developer of the theory of relativity

⸻

If you're not stubborn, you'll give up on experiments too soon. And if you're not flexible, you'll pound your head against the wall and you won't see a different solution to a problem you're trying to solve.

—Jeff Bezos, founder of Amazon.com

⸻

The best way to predict the future is to create it.

—Unknown

Thinking about the bigger picture takes you out of the familiar way of thinking about the problem.
>   —Art Markman, professor of psychology and
>   marketing

———◆———

Great things are not done by impulse, but by a series of small things brought together.
>   —Vincent Van Gogh, artist

———◆———

The great accomplishments of man have resulted from the transmission of ideas of enthusiasm.
>   —Thomas J. Watson, chairman and CEO of IBM

If you want to succeed you should strike out on new paths, rather than travel the worn paths of accepted success.

> —John D. Rockefeller, industrialist, cofounder of Standard Oil Co., and philanthropist

Successful entrepreneurs are able to make great discoveries . . . because they keep alive within themselves the curiosity and wonderment of a small child exploring the universe . . . for the first time.

> —Peter J. Patsula, founder of Patsula Media and author

To think creatively, we must be able to look afresh at what we normally take for granted.

> —George Kneller, philosophy professor

When I examine myself and my methods of thought, I come to the conclusion that the gift of fantasy has meant more to me than any talent for abstract, positive thinking.

—Albert Einstein, developer of the theory of relativity

There is no passion so strong in a man as a desire to learn, when he has reached that plane where he can appreciate the pleasure derived from the attainment of knowledge.

—King Gillette, founder of Gillette Safety Razor Co.

The best way to get a good idea is to have a lot of ideas.

—Linus Pauling, winner of the Nobel Prize in Chemistry and Nobel Peace Prize

Pure mathematics is, in its way, the poetry of logical ideas.

—Albert Einstein, developer of the theory of relativity

The concept is interesting and well-formed, but in order to earn better than a "C," the idea must be feasible.

—Yale professor's comments on FedEx founder Fred Smith's thesis

All the breaks you need in life wait within your imagination; imagination is the workshop of your mind, capable of turning mind energy into accomplishment and wealth.

—Napoleon Hill, pioneer of the modern genre of personal success

Ideas, ideas, ideas—they are the caffeine that keeps us alert.

—Nick Lyons, teacher, writer, and publisher

We are governed not by armies and police, but by ideas.

—Mona Caird, Scottish novelist, essayist, and feminist

Don't worry about people stealing your ideas. If your ideas are any good, you'll have to ram them down people's throats.

—Howard Aiken, physicist and computer pioneer
(as quoted in *Portraits in Silicon,* 1987)

All great deeds and all great thoughts have a ridiculous beginning. Great works are often born on a street corner or in a restaurant's revolving door.

—Albert Camus, French philosopher (from his book *An Absurd Reasoning*)

There's no shortage of remarkable ideas; what's missing is the will to execute them.

—Seth Godin, author, entrepreneur, and public speaker

We live in an age in which superfluous ideas abound and essential ideas are lacking.

—Joseph Joubert, French moralist and essayist

A single idea, if it is right, saves us the labor of an infinity of experiences.

—Jacques Maritain, French Catholic philosopher

Creativity can solve almost any problem. The creative act, the defeat of habit by originality, overcomes everything.

—George Lois, advertising legend

If your brain is a muscle, then it too can get tired out with exercise. How do you exercise it? Thinking.

—Matthew Toren, author, entrepreneur, and investor

Constraint inspired creativity. Blank spaces are difficult to fill, but the smallest prompt can send us in fantastic new directions.

—Biz Stone, cofounder of Twitter

———◆———

We always plan too much and always think too little.

—Joseph Schumpeter, economist and political scientist

———◆———

Nobody talks of entrepreneurship as survival, but that's exactly what it is and what nurtures creative thinking.

—Anita Roddick, founder of the Body Shop

Capital isn't that important in business. Experience isn't that important. You can get both of these things. What is important is ideas.

—Harvey S. Firestone, founder of the Firestone Tire and Rubber Co.

———◆———

Ideas in secret die. They need light and air or they starve to death.

—Seth Godin, author, entrepreneur, and public speaker

Opportunity, Luck, and Change

Opportunity knocks, and the wise businessperson answers the door every time. Leaving opportunity on the table is an invitation for rivals—both businesses and people—to take control. Along with opportunity, luck plays a role in getting ahead. And change, a constant in business, is pregnant with opportunity. For today's business owners and managers to better the chances of survival, the pace of change had better be a never-ending preoccupation. The quotes below offer advice, encouragement, and experience in the area of recognizing opportunity, taking advantage of luck, and mastering change.

In the middle of every difficulty lies opportunity.

—Albert Einstein, developer of the theory of relativity

———◆———

A wise man will make more opportunities than he finds.

—Francis Bacon, English philosopher, statesman, orator, and author

———◆———

Opportunity is manufactured.

—Biz Stone, cofounder of Twitter

Be ready when opportunity comes. . . . Luck is the time when preparation and opportunity meet.

> —Roy D. Chapin Jr., chairman and CEO of American Motors Corp.

In my opinion, neither organisms nor organizations evolve slowly and surely into something better, but drift until some small change occurs which has immediate and overwhelming significance. The special role of the human being is not to wait for these favorable accidents but deliberately to introduce the small change that will have great significance.

> —Dr. Edwin Land, cofounder of the Polaroid Corp.

Opportunity doesn't make appointments; you have to be ready when it arrives.

> —Tim Fargo, CEO of Tweet Jukebox

The sign on the door of opportunity reads PUSH.

—Unknown

You are surrounded by simple, obvious solutions that can dramatically increase your income, power, influence and success. The problem is, you just don't see them.

—Jay Abraham, author and business executive

Nothing is of greater importance than knowing how to make the best use of a good opportunity when it is offered.

—Machiavelli, Italian Renaissance political philosopher

If opportunity doesn't knock, build a door.

—Milton Berle, comedian and actor

———◆———

Few of us can hope to achieve as much as these great men of the past but, no matter how ordinary our endowments, we can at least emulate them by being daring.

—Clarence Birdseye, inventor, entrepreneur, and pioneer of the frozen foods industry

———◆———

The only doors that open are the ones you knock on.

—Scott Marquart, author

I believe in the dignity of labor, whether with head or hand; that the world owes no man a living but that it owes every man an opportunity to make a living.

> —John D. Rockefeller, industrialist, cofounder of Standard Oil Co., and philanthropist

Change is not a threat, it's an opportunity. Survival is not the goal, transformative success is.

> —Seth Godin, author, entrepreneur, and public speaker

Sell a man a fish, he eats for a day, teach a man how to fish, you ruin a wonderful business opportunity.

> —Karl Marx, philosopher, economist, and revolutionary socialist

Try to turn every disaster into an opportunity.

—John D. Rockefeller, industrialist, cofounder of Standard Oil Co., and philanthropist

Business opportunities are like buses; there's always another one coming.

—Sir Richard Branson, billionaire entrepreneur and founder of Virgin Airlines

You've got to seize the opportunity if it is presented to you.

—Clive Davis, music executive

In the midst of chaos, there is also opportunity.

—Sun Tzu, Chinese general, military strategist, and philosopher

You've got to look for a gap, where competitors in a market have grown lazy and lost contact with the readers or the viewers.

—Rupert Murdoch, media mogul

Saying no to loud people gives you the resources to say yes to important opportunities.

—Seth Godin, author, entrepreneur, and public speaker

If someone funded your company, they funded your ideas and vision; your job is to turn that capital into the thing that's in your head.

—Dennis Crowley, CEO of Foursquare

Luck is a dividend of sweat. The more you sweat, the luckier you get.

—Ray Kroc, chairman of McDonald's

I'm a great believer in luck and I find the harder I work, the more I have of it.

—Stephen Leacock, Canadian teacher, political scientist, writer, and humorist

321

In every life there is a moment—an event or a realization—that changes that life irrevocably. If the change is to be a happy one, one must be able to recognize the moment and seize it without delay.

—Estée Lauder, cofounder of Estée Lauder Companies

There is no security on the earth, there is only opportunity.

—Gen. Douglas MacArthur, US military leader

I'm a catalyst for change. You can't be an outsider and be successful over 30 years without leaving a certain amount of scar tissue around the place.

—Rupert Murdoch, media mogul

If you think of [opportunity] in terms of Gold Rush, then you'd be pretty depressed right now because the last nugget of gold would be gone. But the good thing is, with innovation, there isn't a last nugget. Every new thing creates two new questions and two new opportunities.

— Jeff Bezos, founder of Amazon.com

———✦———

Life is a series of natural and spontaneous changes. Don't resist them; that only creates sorrow. Let reality be reality. Let things flow naturally forward in whatever way they like.

— Lao Tzu, philosopher and writer

———✦———

People always fear change. People feared electricity when it was invented, didn't they? People feared coal, they feared gas-powered engines. . . . There will always be ignorance, and ignorance leads to fear. But with time, people will come to accept their silicon masters.

— Bill Gates, cofounder of Microsoft and
   philanthropist

Man is emotional, and quickly carried forward upon waves of popular excitement; and it is these great tidal waves of emotion that mark the revolutionary changes throughout history.

—King Gillette, founder of Gillette Safety Razor Co.

———

Opportunity + Preparation = Luck. . , . People see other's successes and they think, oh, they're just lucky. Nobody is ever lucky, trust me. Sure, things happen to people. There's stories everywhere of people who've been toiling away and all of a sudden, they get the dream job they've always wanted; or their business idea suddenly takes off and they make millions. We look at that and think, they're lucky. No honey, they're not lucky. They were prepared.

—As told to Betty Liu by her television coach

———

It is not the strongest of the species that survive, nor the most intelligent, but the one most responsive to change.

—Charles Darwin, developer of the theory of evolution

Change will not come if we wait for some other person or some other time. We are the ones we've been waiting for. We are the change that we seek.

—Barack Obama, US president

Productivity

Work hard, get ahead. Be smart about how you work. Value your time. Know how to start and when to finish. Today's workers face numerous challenges to productivity—the least of which is technology, which can distract them as well as propel them forward. Managers face similar challenges in terms of the productivity of their employees. Learn from the people below how to get moving and stay productive.

I'm not into fame. I'm not into making money, outside of financing my books. I'm not into status. My thing is basically about time—not wasting it.

> —Henry Rollins, musician, actor, television and radio
> host, and comedian

You are not your resume, you are your work.

> —Seth Godin, author, entrepreneur, and public speaker

You're better off with a kick-ass half than a half-assed whole.

> —David Heinemeier Hansson, Danish computer
> programmer

All glory comes from daring to begin.

—Eugene F. Ware, author

Either write something worth reading or do something worth writing.

—Benjamin Franklin, US founding father and inventor

The general who wins the battle makes many calculations in his temple before the battle is fought. The general who loses makes but few calculations beforehand.

—Sun Tzu, Chinese general, military strategist, and philosopher

Often, we're so focused on what we haven't done that we can't accurately see our progress.

— Marci G. Fox, psychologist

Don't wait. The time will never be just right.

— Napoleon Hill, pioneer of the modern genre of personal success

---

Employees who report receiving recognition and praise within the last seven days show increased productivity, get higher scores from customers, and have better safety records. They're just more engaged at work.

— Tom Rath, author

Therefore, to maximize your productivity, deliberately focus on precisely one thing at a time.

—Oran Kangas, author

———◆———

Happiness is found in doing, not merely possessing.

—Napoleon Hill, pioneer of the modern genre
of personal success

———◆———

I always had the uncomfortable feeling that if I wasn't sitting in front of a computer typing, I was wasting my time—but I pushed myself to take a wider view of what was "productive." Time spent with my family and friends was never wasted.

—Gretchen Rubin, author, blogger, and speaker

Cell phones, mobile e-mail, and all the other cool and slick gadgets can cause massive losses in our creative output and overall productivity.

—Robert S. Sharma, Canadian self-help writer

There's no "right time" to take the leap; you can take it at any point in your life, and should.

—Rehan Choudhry, founder of Life Is Beautiful, Las Vegas music festival

We generate fears while we sit. We overcome them by action. Fear is nature's way of warning us to get busy.

—Dr. Henry Link, employment psychologist

Part of being a winner is knowing when enough is enough. Sometimes you have to give up the fight and walk away. Move on to something else that's more productive.

> —Donald Trump, real estate developer, author, and presidential candidate

---

It is the greatest of all mistakes to do nothing because you can only do a little. Do what you can.

> —Sydney Smith, English essayist

Know the true value of time! Snatch, seize, and enjoy every moment of it. No idleness, no laziness, no procrastination. Never put off till tomorrow what you can do today.

> —Lord Chesterfield Stanhope, British statesman and man of letters

Putting off an easy thing makes it hard. Putting off a hard thing makes it impossible.

—George Claude Lorimer, pastor

———◆———

Authority—when abused through micromanagement, intimidation, or verbal or nonverbal threats—makes people shut down and productivity ceases.

—John Stoker, author

———◆———

The simple act of paying positive attention to people has a great deal to do with productivity.

—Tom Peters, author and business management expert

. . . If you're not getting told "no" enough times a day, you're probably not doing it right or you're probably not pushing yourself hard enough.
    —Shafqat Islam, CEO of NewsCred

———✦———

I enjoy writing, I enjoy my house, my family and, more than anything I enjoy the feeling of seeing each day used to the full to actually produce something. The end.
    —Michael Palin, English comedian, actor, and writer

———✦———

Just Redo It.
    —Peter J. Patsula, founder of Patsula Media and author

Knowing is not enough, we must apply. Willing is not enough, we must do.

—Johann Von Goethe, German writer and statesman

Times of great calamity and confusion have been productive for the greatest minds. The purest ore is produced from the hottest furnace. The brightest thunder-bolt is elicited from the darkest storm.

—Charles Caleb Colton, English cleric, writer, and collector

Why do anything unless it is going to be great?

—Peter Block, author and business consultant

If things seem under control, you are just not going fast enough.

—Mario Andretti, racing driver

Cease to think of an impossibility and you will seize an opportunity for productivity. Excellence comes when you leave thoughts of impossibilities behind and live by the focus of faith and hope in the face of difficulty.

—Israelmore Ayivor, writer

Productivity is never an accident. It is always the result of a commitment to excellence, intelligent planning, and focused effort.

—Paul J. Meyer, founder of Success Motivation
Institute

Understanding your employee's perspective can go a long way towards increasing productivity and happiness.

—Kathryn Minshew, CEO and cofounder of The Muse

It's not always that we need to do more but rather that we need to focus on less.

—Nathan W. Morris, author and personal finance expert

Youth is an unpleasant period; for then it is not possible or not prudent to be productive in any sense whatsoever.

—Friedrich Nietzsche, German philosopher, cultural critic, and poet

Resist the short term temptation of procrastination; the immediate pleasure and relief that it brings does not fare in comparison to the long lasting damage it does to your dreams and goals.

> —Noel DeJesus, author (from his book *44 Day of Leadership*, 2013)

Work is a process, and any process needs to be controlled. To make work productive, therefore, requires building the appropriate controls into the process of work.

> —Peter F. Drucker, management consultant, educator, and author

Don't interpret anything too much. This is time waster Number 1.

> —Dee Dee Artner, author and behavioral expert

If you had to identify, in one word, the reason why the human race has not achieved, and never will achieve, its full potential, that word would be "meetings."

—Dave Barry, author and columnist

Anyone can do any amount of work, provided it isn't the work he is supposed to be doing at that moment.

—Robert Benchley, author

Peak productivity is the result of dedication and awareness.

—Peter Voogd, media entrepreneur and author

You may delay, but time will not.

—Benjamin Franklin, US founding father and inventor

———◆◆———

But I was too restless to watch long; I'm too Occidental for a long vigil. I could work at a problem for years, but to wait inactive for twenty-four hours—that's another matter.

—H. G. Wells, English writer

———◆◆———

Today my goal is to be more productive than I was yesterday, and tomorrow more productive than today.

—Noel DeJesus, author (from his book *44 Day of Leadership*, 2013)

Like any other tool for facilitating the completion of a questionable task, rewards offer a "how" answer to what is really a "why" question.

—Alfie Kohn, author and lecturer

Nothing is less productive than to make more efficient what should not be done at all.

—Peter F. Drucker, management consultant, educator, and author

---

If everyone in America started mailing empty boxes, we could boost productivity, profitability, and employment. Think like a politician.

—Jarod Kintz, author

Many companies have long contended that stress in the home causes productivity loss in the market place . . . and it does. But research now reveals that stress on the job causes stress at home. In other words, they feed off each other.

—Zig Ziglar, motivational speaker

—◆◆—

My goal is no longer to get more done, but rather to have less to do.

—Francine Jay, author and minimalist

—◆◆—

Productivity is being able to do things that you were never able to do before.

—Franz Kafka, novelist and short story writer

We just have to go at 100 miles an hour in all our businesses, be they television broadcasting, be they magazine publishing, be they subscription television, be they online, be they gaming. We just have to go at one hundred miles an hour.

—James Parker, contributing editor, Atlantic magazine

Take time to stop and re-focus your priorities as often as needed. Intelligent thinking, combined with the right action, will get your productivity to a level few attain.

—Peter Voogd, media entrepreneur and author

Procrastination is the fear of success. People procrastinate because they are afraid of the success that they know will result if they move ahead now. Because success is heavy, carries a responsibility with it, it is much easier to procrastinate and live on the "someday I'll" philosophy.

—Denis Waitley, motivational speaker, writer, and consultant

Multitasking is a lie.

—Gary Keller, author

———◆———

We all get report cards in many different ways, but the real excitement of what you're doing is in the doing of it. It's not what you're gonna get in the end—it's not the final curtain—it's really in the doing it, and loving what I'm doing. That's my high. What's next? I don't know. I'm just doing it.

—Ralph Lauren, fashion designer

———◆———

You may hate to disappoint people, but for your own productivity, learn how to say "no" to people. It isn't always the greatest feeling, but it is impossible to appease everyone.

—Jonathan Long, founder and CEO of Market Domination Media

Procrastination is the bad habit of putting off until the day after tomorrow what should have been done the day before yesterday.

—Napoleon Hill, pioneer of the modern genre of personal success

The great end of life is not knowledge but action.

—Thomas Huxley, English biologist

Success

Businesspeople are consumed with the urgent matter of succeeding. Whether they're looking for the secret to success, a formula for success, or ways around obstacles to success, the topic is always top of mind. No matter the definition of success—money, personal satisfaction, social good—the quotes here will help success seekers thrive.

If you don't do it excellently, don't do it at all. Because if it's not excellent, it won't be profitable or fun, and if you're not in business for fun or profit, what the hell are you doing there?

—Robert Townsend, author (from his book *Up the Organization,* 2007)

The three great essentials to achieve anything worthwhile are, first, hard work; second, stick-to-itiveness; third, common sense.

—Thomas Edison, inventor

Something in human nature causes us to start slacking off at our moment of greatest accomplishment. As you become successful, you will need a great deal of self-discipline not to lose your sense of balance, humility, and commitment.

—Ross Perot, businessman and Reform Party presidential candidate

Success comes from keeping the ears open and the mouth closed.

—John D. Rockefeller, industrialist, cofounder of Standard Oil Co., and philanthropist

——◆——

Always do what you say you are going to do. It is the glue and fiber that binds successful relationships.

—Jeffry A. Timmons, professor of entrepreneurship

——◆——

If you work hard, and become successful, it does not necessarily mean you are successful because you worked hard, just as if you are tall with long hair it doesn't mean that you would be a midget if you were bald.

— Daniel Handler, author and journalist

349

People who succeed have momentum. The more they succeed, the more they want to succeed, and the more they find a way to succeed. Similarly, when someone is failing, the tendency is to get on a downward spiral that can even become a self-fulfilling prophecy.

—Tony Robbins, motivational speaker, personal finance instructor, and self-help author

Would you like me to give you a formula for success? It's quite simple, really: Double your rate of failure. You are thinking of failure as the enemy of success. But it isn't at all. You can be discouraged by failure or you can learn from it, so go ahead and make mistakes. Make all you can. Because remember that's where you will find success.

—Thomas J. Watson, chairman and CEO of IBM

Patience, persistence and perspiration make an unbeatable combination for success.

—Napoleon Hill, pioneer of the modern genre of personal success

Recipe for success: Be polite, prepare yourself for whatever you are asked to do, keep yourself tidy, be cheerful, don't be envious, be honest with yourself so you will be honest with others, be helpful, interest yourself in your job, don't pity yourself, be quick to praise, be loyal to your friends, avoid prejudices, be independent, interest yourself in politics, and read the newspapers.

—Bernard Baruch, financier, stock investor, philanthropist, and statesman

I made a resolve then that I was going to amount to something if I could. And no hours, nor amount of labor, nor amount of money would deter me from giving the best that there was in me. And I have done that ever since, and I win by it.

—Colonel Sanders, founder of Kentucky Fried Chicken

Show up early. Work hard. Stay late. Work eight hours and sleep eight hours, and make sure that they are not the same eight hours.

—T. Boone Pickens, Texas oilman and investor

Just Do It.
—Nike, athletic shoe company

━━◆◆◆━━

Life is a series of experiences, each one of which makes us bigger, even though sometimes it is hard to realize this. For the world was built to develop character, and we must learn that the setbacks and grieves which we endure help us in our marching onward.
—Henry Ford, founder of Ford Motor Co.

━━◆◆◆━━

When I dare to be powerful—to use my strength in the service of my vision, then it becomes less and less important whether I am afraid.
—Audre Lorde, writer, feminist, and civil rights activist

You've achieved success in your field when you don't know whether what you're doing is work or play.

    —Warren Beatty, actor

———◆◆◆———

Success or failure depends more upon attitude than upon capacity. Successful men act as though they have accomplished or are enjoying something. Soon it becomes a reality. Act, look, feel successful, conduct yourself accordingly, and you will be amazed at the positive results.

    —William James, philosopher and psychologist (from his book *The Principles of Psychology,* 1890)

———◆◆◆———

Yesterday's home runs don't win today's games.

    —Babe Ruth, baseball legend

The toughest thing about success is that you've got to keep on being a success.

—Irving Berlin, composer

Success is often the result of taking a misstep in the right direction.

—Al Bernstein, journalist and sportscaster

A successful man is one who can lay a firm foundation with the bricks others have thrown at him.

—David Brinkley, news anchor for NBC and ABC

Successful people maintain a positive focus in life no matter what is going on around them. They stay focused on their past successes rather than their past failures, and on the next action steps they need to take to get them closer to the fulfillment of their goals rather than all the other distractions that life presents to them.

—Jack Canfield, author and entrepreneur

Success is the sum of small efforts—repeated day in and day out.

—Robert Collier, self-help author

The feeding trough in America is endless. Everyone can step up. All you have to do is work hard and take advantage of the opportunities you're given.

—T. Boone Pickens, Texas oilman and investor

I believe that being successful means having a balance of success stories across the many areas of your life. You can't truly be considered successful in your business life if your home life is in shambles.

—Zig Ziglar, motivational speaker

All successful people have a goal. No one can get anywhere unless he knows where he wants to go and what he wants to be or do.

—Norman Vincent Peale, minister, author, and a pioneer of "positive thinking"

I believe the only way to succeed is to keep getting ahead all the time.

—John D. Rockefeller, industrialist, cofounder of Standard Oil Co., and philanthropist

It took ten years to understand that "All of our successes have not just been luck. . . ."

—Danny Meyer, restaurant entrepreneur

I don't like to show all my cards too early . . . and that gives me two distinct advantages: my opponents often get the wrong read on me, and I push myself longer and harder.

—T. Boone Pickens, Texas oilman and investor

To be successful, you have to be able to relate to people; they have to be satisfied with your personality to be able to do business with you and to build a relationship with mutual trust.

—George Ross, Trump Organization executive

Men are born to succeed, not to fail.

> —Henry David Thoreau, author, poet, philosopher,
> abolitionist, and naturalist

—◆—

Success in life is what you do with your ideas and vision.
While action is important, the first step of success deals
with training your mind.

> —Matthew Toren, author, entrepreneur, and investor

—◆—

Success is simply a matter of luck. Ask any failure.

> —Earl Nightingale, radio personality, writer, and
> author

Success in business requires training and discipline and hard work. But if you're not frightened by these things, the opportunities are just as great today as they ever were.

—David Rockefeller, banker

———◆———

I am aware that success is more than a good idea. It is timing too.

—Anita Roddick, founder of the Body Shop (from AnitaRoddick.com)

———◆———

The secret of success is to do the common things uncommonly well.

—John D. Rockefeller, industrialist, cofounder of Standard Oil Co., and philanthropist

The successful warrior is the average man, with laser-like focus.

—Bruce Lee, actor

———◆———

Success is getting what you want, happiness is wanting what you get.

—W. P. Kinsella, novelist and short story writer

———◆———

Successful companies are built by investing large amount of money and hundreds of litres of sweat.

—Amit Kalantri, author

Success is not a destination, but the road that you're on. Being successful means that you're working hard and walking your walk every day. You can only live your dream by working hard towards it. That's living your dream.

—Marlon Wayans, actor and comedian

Businesses are successful because someone makes the sacrifices others are unwilling to.

—Kijung Kim, South Korean badminton player

Integrity is the essence of everything successful.

—R. Buckminster Fuller, architect, systems theorist, author, designer, and inventor

Success is liking yourself, liking what you do, and liking how you do it.

—Maya Angelou, author and poet

———◆———

You aren't going to find anybody that's going to be successful without making a sacrifice and without perseverance.

—Lou Holtz, college basketball coaching legend

———◆———

Before everything else, getting ready is the secret of success.

—Henry Ford, founder of Ford Motor Co.

A business is successful to the extent that it provides a product or service that contributes to happiness in all of its forms.

—Mihaly Csikszentmihalyi, Hungarian psychologist

———◆———

There are a lot of things that go into creating success. I don't like to do just the things I like to do. I like to do things that cause the company to succeed. I don't spend a lot of time doing my favorite activities.

—Michael Dell, founder of Dell Computers

———◆———

The secret of success is consistency of purpose.

—Benjamin Disraeli, British prime minister and writer

If somebody can do something at least 80 percent as well as you, make it their job. Your time is more valuable. I've never met a successful person who doesn't value their time, and I've never met an average person who did.

—Peter Voogd, media entrepreneur and author

Success has a simple formula: do your best, and people may like it.

—Sam Ewing, professional baseball player

As I've progressed in my career, I've come to appreciate—and really value—the other attributes that define a company's success beyond the P&L: great leadership, long-term financial strength, ethical business practices, evolving business strategies, sound governance, powerful brands, values-based decision making.

—Ursula Burns, CEO of Xerox

Strive not to be a success, but rather to be of value.

—Albert Einstein, developer of the theory of relativity

These three things, will power, work, and success, are the mainstays of human existence: will power opens the doors to brilliant and happy careers; work allows us to pass through them, and once we have run the course, success will crown our achievement.

—Louis Pasteur, chemist and investor of pasteurization

It's possible—you can never know—that the universe exists only for me. If so, it's sure going well for me, I must admit.

—Bill Gates, cofounder of Microsoft and philanthropist

365

I've always believed that one woman's success can only help another woman's success.

—Gloria Vanderbilt, fashion designer

The only place success comes before work is in the dictionary.

—Vidal Sassoon, hair care mogul

Winning is not a sometime thing; it's an all time thing. You don't win once in a while, you don't do things right once in a while, you do them right all the time. Winning is habit. Unfortunately, so is losing.

—Vince Lombardi, legendary professional football coach

Action is the foundational key to all success.
—Pablo Picasso, artist

❦

It's only when we can work with something that brings out our strengths that we're of any real use.
—Henning Mankell, Swedish crime writer (from *The Fifth Woman*, 2000)

❦

Successful people are the ones who are breaking the rules.
—Seth Godin, author, entrepreneur, and public speaker

When deliberating, think in campaigns and not battles; in wars and not campaigns; in ultimate conquest and not wars.

—Steven Pressfield, author

I've come to believe that each of us has a personal calling that's as unique as a fingerprint—and that the best way to succeed is to discover what you love and then find a way to offer it to others in the form of service, working hard, and also allowing the energy of the universe to lead you.

—Oprah Winfrey, media mogul, television host, and actress

When I was a child my mother said to me, "If you become a soldier, you'll be a general. If you become a monk, you'll be the pope." Instead I became a painter and wound up as Picasso.

—Pablo Picasso, artist

Teamwork and Leadership

That "two heads are better than one"—in a word, teamwork—often is the most difficult concept to drill into the collective head of a labor force. Just ask any business owner or manager. The task entails convincing individuals to subordinate personal ambition, something that seems to be extremely counterintuitive in today's super-competitive, what's-in-it-for-me economy. The idea of teamwork is anathema even to team occupations. The professional football, basketball, or baseball player who doesn't secretly (or not so secretly) hope to be his or her team's standout performer may not exist. Anyone tasked with cobbling individual workers into perfect alignment needs to tout the virtues of teamwork—and display attributes of leadership at the same time.

No manager can have too much knowledge about a business or those who work for him. . . .

—Nick Lyons, teacher, writer, and publisher

———◆———

Really in technology, it's about the people, retaining them, nurturing a creative environment and helping to find a way to innovate.

—Marissa Mayer, CEO of Yahoo!

———◆———

Any great building will never stand if you neglect the small bricks.

—Ifeanyi Enoch Onuoha, author, inspirational speaker, and life coach

The reaction of weak management to weak operations is often weak accounting.

—Warren Buffett, legendary investor and CEO of Berkshire Hathaway

Every company has two organizational structures: The formal one is written on the charts; the other is the everyday relationship of the men and women in the organization.

—Harold S. Geneen, chairman of ITT Corp.

Fewer employees will be loyal to a firm than will be loyal to a specific manager.

—Nick Lyons, teacher, writer, and publisher

I've been convinced my entire business career, that I need my employees more than they need me.

—Steve Wynn, casino owner

"Restore connection" is not just for devices, it is for people too. If we cannot disconnect, we cannot lead. Creating the culture of burnout is opposite to creating a culture of sustainable creativity. This is something that needs to be taught in business schools. This mentality needs to be introduced as a leadership and performance-enhancing tool.

—Arianna Huffington, founder of the *Huffington Post*

Leaders teach. They motivate. They care. Leaders make sure that the way to success is always broad enough and straight enough for others to follow.

—Mary Kay Ash, founder of Mary Kay Cosmetics

To succeed in business, it is necessary to make others see things as you see them.
—John H. Patterson, National Cash Register Co.

If ethics are poor at the top, that behavior is copied down through the organization.
—Robert Noyce, cofounder of Fairchild Semiconductor and Intel Corp.

A company has a greater responsibility than making money for its stockholders. We have a responsibility to our employees to recognize their dignity as human beings.
—David Packard, cofounder of Hewlett-Packard

The glue that holds all relationships together—including the relationship between the leader and the led—is trust, and trust is based on integrity.

—Brian Tracy, author

It is easier to hire a friend than it is to manage . . . or fire a friend.

—Nick Lyons, teacher, writer, and publisher

Objectives are not fate; they are direction. They are not commands; they are commitments. They do not determine the future; they are means to mobilize the resources and energies of the business for the making of the future.

—Peter F. Drucker, management consultant, educator, and author

To understand KKR, I always like to say, don't congratulate us when we buy a company. Any fool can buy a company. Congratulate us when we sell it and when we've done something with it and created real value.

 —Henry Kravis, cofounder of Kohlberg Kravis Roberts & Co.

With our technology, with objects, literally three people in a garage can blow away what 200 people at Microsoft can do. Literally can blow it away. Corporate America has a need that is so huge and can save them so much money, or make them so much money, or cost them so much money if they miss it, that they are going to fuel the object revolution.

 —Steve Jobs, cofounder of Apple and Pixar Animation

I am especially thankful that I learned early to take an interest in other fields than business, so when I was able to shift more and more active business cares from my shoulders to those of other men I could do so without regret for I had other fields of activity awaiting my attention which have proved of absorbing interest.

—John D. Rockefeller, industrialist, cofounder of Standard Oil Co., and philanthropist

I asked the CEO of Time Warner, "What is the skill that is most valuable in business that doesn't get taught in the classroom?" He said teamwork. Making people want to work with you. That explains why some people get promotions, or funding, etc. And other people don't.

—Fareed Zakaria, CNN host and *New York Times* bestselling author

My quest to find, and be surrounded by, smart people is what brought me to Google.

—Marissa Mayer, CEO of Yahoo!

In business for yourself, not by yourself.

—William James, philosopher and psychologist (from his book *The Principles of Psychology*, 1890)

———◆———

Work with your competitors when the interest of the community and planet are at stake.

—Simon Mainwaring, branding consultant, advertising creative director, and social media expert

———◆———

Business, labor and civil society organizations have skills and resources that are vital in helping to build a more robust global community.

—Kofi Annan, secretary-general of the United Nations

377

In terms of doing work and in terms of learning and evolving as a person, you just grow more when you get more people's perspectives.

—Mark Zuckerberg, cofounder and CEO of Facebook

Salespeople, leaders, entrepreneurs and business people are full of ideas . . . about how to make the world a better place, make money, solve problems and lots more. But the very nature of active listening requires us to put aside our ideas completely, if only for a moment, in order to focus on what someone else has to say.

—Dave Kerpen, entrepreneur, author, and reality television personality

I may not be the smartest fellow in the world, but I can sure pick the smartest people to do business with and size them up very fast.

—Ziad K. Abdelnour, investment banker and financier

If you want to go quickly, go alone. If you want to go far, go together.

—African Proverb

———◆◆———

Team spirit promotes greater accomplishment.

—Lailah Gifty Akita, founder of Smart Youth Volunteers Foundation

———◆◆———

It takes two flints to make a fire.

—Louisa May Alcott, novelist and poet

Sticks in a bundle are unbreakable.

—Bondei proverb

None of us is as smart as all of us.

—Ken Blanchard, author and management expert

It's feeling the sense of responsibility, the sense of ownership, to step in, to try to solve any problem—and the humility to step back and embrace the better ideas of others. Your end goal, is what can we do together to problem-solve. I've contributed my piece, and then I step back.

—Laszlo Bock, Google executive

What we care about is, when faced with a problem and you're a member of a team, do you, at the appropriate time, step in and lead? And just as critically, do you step back and stop leading, do you let someone else?

    —Laszlo Bock, Google executive

Only by binding together as a single force will we remain strong and unconquerable.

    —Chris Bradford, author, professional musician, and black belt martial artist

---

Respect your fellow human being, treat them fairly, disagree with them honestly, enjoy their friendship, explore your thoughts about one another candidly, work together for a common goal and help one another achieve it.

    —Bill Bradley, NBA star and US senator

In order to have a winner, the team must have a feeling of unity; every player must put the team first ahead of personal glory.

—Paul Bear Bryant, legendary Alabama football coach

Cooperation is the thorough conviction that nobody can get there unless everybody gets there.

—Virginia Burden Tower, author

Today's organizations thrive when they maximize what they know. Results depend on the collective talents and creativity of people.

—Evangeline Caridas, consultant

Teamwork is the ability to work together toward a common vision. The ability to direct individual accomplishments toward organizational objectives. It is the fuel that allows common people to attain uncommon results.
—Andrew Carnegie, steel industrialist

All of us, at certain moments of our lives, need to take advice and to receive help from other people.
—Alexis Carrel, French surgeon and biologist

The nice thing about teamwork is that you always have others on your side.
—Margaret Carty, Oregon politician

If we are together nothing is impossible. If we are divided all will fail.

—Winston Churchill, former prime minister of the United Kingdom

I don't know where we should take this company, but I do know that if I start with the right people, ask them the right questions, and engage them in vigorous debate, we will find a way to make this company great.

—Jim Collins, business consultant, author, and lecturer

I invite everyone to choose forgiveness rather than division, teamwork over personal ambition.

—John-Francois Cope, French politician

Interdependent people combine their own efforts with the efforts of others to achieve their greatest success.

—Stephen Covey, educator, author, and businessman

———◆———

You put together the best team that you can with the players you've got, and replace those who aren't good enough.

—Robert Crandall, airline executive

———◆———

...[C]urate the team to make sure the people who are great stay, and the people who aren't as good get the help they need to become great.

—Dennis Crowley, Internet executive

In the long history of humankind (and animal kind, too) those who learned to collaborate and improvise most effectively have prevailed.

—Charles Darwin, developer of the theory of evolution

What we need to do is learn to work in the system, by which I mean that everybody, every team, every platform, every division, every component is there not for individual competitive profit or recognition, but for contribution to the system as a whole on a win-win basis.

—W. Edwards Deming, engineer, scholar, author, and management consultant

You will find men who want to be carried on the shoulders of others, who think that the world owes them a living. They don't seem to see that we must all lift together and pull together.

—Henry Ford, founder of Ford Motor Co.

People have been known to achieve more as a result of working with others than against them.

—D. Allan Fromme, psychologist, teacher, and writer

———◆———

Teamwork makes the dream work.

—Bang Gae, music producer

———◆———

Coming together is a beginning. Keeping together is progress. Working together is success.

—Henry Ford, founder of Ford Motor Co.

One thing I've always loved about the culture at Microsoft is there is nobody who is tougher on us, in terms of what we need to learn and do better, than the people in the company itself. You can walk down these halls, and they'll tell you, "We need to do usability better, push this or that frontier."

—Bill Gates, cofounder of Microsoft and
philanthropist

The question I ask myself like almost every day is, "Am I doing the most important thing I could be doing?"... Unless I feel that I'm working on the most important problem that I can help with, then I'm not going to feel good about how I'm spending my time.

—Mark Zuckerberg, cofounder and CEO of Facebook

I'd rather have 1 percent of the efforts of 100 people than 100 percent of my own efforts.

—J. Paul Getty, founder of Getty Oil Co.

No matter what accomplishments you make, somebody helped you.

—Althea Gibson, pioneer black tennis player

———◆———

There are few, if any, jobs in which ability alone is sufficient. Needed, also, are loyalty, sincerity, enthusiasm and team play.

—William B. Given Jr., author

———◆———

A team is more than a collection of people. It is a process of give and take.

—Barbara Glacel, executive coach

If everyone is moving forward together, then success takes care of itself.

—Henry Ford, founder of Ford Motor Co.

I am a member of a team, and I rely on the team, I defer to it and sacrifice for it, because the team, not the individual, is the ultimate champion.

—Mia Hamm, professional soccer player

Contrary to popular belief, there most certainly is an "I" in "team." It is the same "I" that appears three times in "responsibility."

—Amber Harding, multimedia sports journalist

Many hands make light work.

    —John Heywood, English playwright

❖

Teamwork is a make or break situation. Either you help make it or the lack of it will break you.

    —Kris A. Hiatt, author

❖

There is something about building up a comradeship—that I still believe is the greatest of all feats—and sharing in the dangers with your company of peers. It's the intense effort, the giving of everything you've got. It's really a very pleasant sensation.

    —Edmund Hillary, New Zealand mountaineer,
      explorer, and philanthropist

391

Light is the task where many share the toil.
—Homer, Greek poet

Teamwork: Easier said than done.
—Nauman Faridi, Internet technologist

When you form a team, why do you try to form a team?
Because teamwork builds trust and trust builds speed.
—Russel Honore, US military officer

One man can be a crucial ingredient on a team, but one man cannot make a team.
　　　—Kareem Abdul-Jabbar, NBA star

The strength of the team is each individual member. The strength of each member is the team.
　　　—Phil Jackson, NBA coach and team executive

My model for business is The Beatles. They were four guys who kept each other's kind of negative tendencies in check. They balanced each other and the total was greater than the sum of the parts. That's how I see business: great things in business are never done by one person, they're done by a team of people.
　　　—Steve Jobs, cofounder of Apple and Pixar Animation

Your team is one of your most important investments . . . and if you are careful about hiring only the best people, it will pay dividends.

> —Sheila Johnson, cofounder of Black Entertainment Television

———◦◦———

Even the strongest, most well-built team will, at times, be met with adversity. What makes us great is not that we should anticipate less adversity the stronger that we become, but rather that in anticipation of adversity we become stronger.

> —Michael Joling, author

———◦◦———

To collaborative team members, completing one another is more important than competing with one another.

> —John C. Maxwell, author, speaker, and pastor

Talent wins games, but teamwork and intelligence wins championships.
—Michael Jordan, NBA legend

Leadership happens at every level of the organization and no one can shirk from this responsibility.
—Jerry Junkins, CEO of Texas Instruments

Alone we can do so little; together we can do so much.
—Helen Keller, journalist, author, and activist for the blind

The difference between success and failure is a great team.

> —Dave Kerpen, entrepreneur, author, and reality television personality

———◆———

Team player: One who unites others toward a shared destiny through sharing information and ideas, empowering others and developing trust.

> —Dennis Kinlaw, theological educator

———◆———

I love teamwork. I love the idea of everyone rallying together to help me win.

> —Jarod Kintz, author

We're a team. It's part of our job to help each other out, and to forgive each other quickly. Otherwise, we'd never get anything done.

—Jeramey Kraatz, author

To me, teamwork is the beauty of our sport, where you have five acting as one. You become selfless.

—Mike Krzyzewski, college basketball coach

Remember teamwork begins by building trust. And the only way to do that is to overcome our need for invulnerability.

—Patrick Lencioni, author and management expert

Twelve years, two companies, 100 employees, and three times on the Inc. 500 list of fastest-growing companies later, I've learned that the only way to build a company with great success and scale is to build a great team.

> —Dave Kerpen, entrepreneur, author, and reality television personality

Overwhelmed? Delegate. For perfectionists of the world, this is often a challenge. While you may think only you can do it best, you are denying someone else an opportunity to learn when you do everything yourself. Being the bottleneck serves no one, including you.

> —Lisa A. Mininni, author

The greater the loyalty of a group toward the group, the greater is the motivation among the members to achieve the goals of the group, and the greater the probability that the group will achieve its goals.

> —Rensis Likert, social psychologist

Individual commitment to a group effort—that is what makes a team work, a company work, a society work, a civilization work.

—Vince Lombardi, legendary professional coach

<hr />

If you have a team or staff at your disposal, utilize them. Many entrepreneurs are so stubborn and think they can do it all. Delegating appropriate tasks will free up your time.

—Jonathan Long, entrepreneur

<hr />

The greatest danger a team faces isn't that it won't become successful, but that it will, and then cease to improve.

—Mark Sanborn, author and entrepreneur

No one can whistle a symphony. It takes an orchestra to play it.

—H. E. Luccock, author

———◆◆◆———

I find it fascinating that a snowflake, by itself, can be so delicate; but when they team up, they can close down an entire city.

—Steve Maraboli, author and behavioral scientist

———◆◆◆———

Teamwork makes the dream work, but a vision becomes a nightmare when the leader has a big dream and a bad team.

—John C. Maxwell, author, speaker, and pastor

Strategy is not really a solo sport—even if you're the CEO.

—Max McKeown, English writer and consultant

———◆———

Trust is knowing that when a team member does push you, they're doing it because they care about the team.

—Patrick Lencioni, author and management expert

———◆———

Never doubt that a small group of thoughtful, committed people can change the world. Indeed, it is the only thing that ever has.

—Margaret Mead, anthropologist

Projects become complex because we try to solve it alone. Use your working relationships to help you problem-solve. Your solution may be as easy as asking your online community for help and direction.

> —Lisa A. Mininni, author

Creating teams that have an understanding of not only what they are doing but, most important, why they are doing it, is critical.

> —Jim Murren, chairman and CEO of MGM Resorts International

We = power

> —Lorii Myers, author

If I have seen further than others, it is by standing upon the shoulders of giants.

—Isaac Newton, English physicist and mathematician

———◆———

Nobody can achieve success alone.

—Ifeanyi Enoch Onuoha, author, inspirational speaker, and life coach

———◆———

If you can laugh together, you can work together.

—Robert Orben, comedy writer

The best teamwork comes from men who are working independently toward one goal in unison.

—J. C. Penney, founder of retail chain JCPenney

No man is wise enough by himself.

—Titus Maccius Plautus, Roman playwright

Although individuals need not be well-rounded, teams should be.

—Tom Rath, author

Collaboration, it turns out, is not a gift from the gods but a skill that requires effort and practice.
—Douglas B. Reeves, education author

———✦———

Build for your team a feeling of oneness, of dependence on one another and of strength to be derived by unity.
—Vince Lombardi, legendary professional football coach

———✦———

Research has found that in most companies managers who get promoted rapidly spend most of their time networking and politicking, while their more effective colleagues spent their time building their units and developing their people.
—Alan G. Robinson, business executive

The work of the individual still remains the spark that moves mankind ahead even more than teamwork.

—Igor Sikorsky, Russian-American aviation pioneer

———

What a great boon it is to a man—to have another man tell him that he believes in him, that he trusts him! What a happiness all my business experience has been because my associates believed in me, trusted me implicitly!

—John D. Rockefeller, industrialist, cofounder of Standard Oil Co., and philanthropist

———

The way a team plays as a whole determines its success.

—Babe Ruth, baseball legend

Every successful individual knows that his or her achievement depends on a community of persons working together.

> —Paul Ryan, speaker of the US House of
> Representatives

—◆—

In teamwork, silence isn't golden, it's deadly.

> —Mark Sanborn, author and entrepreneur

—◆—

Individually, we are one drop. Together, we are an ocean.

> —Ryunosuke Satoro, Japanese writer

A few harmless flakes working together can unleash an avalanche of destruction.

—Justin Sewell, author

With an enthusiastic team you can achieve almost anything.

—Tahir Shah, Anglo-Afghan Indian author and journalist

It is much more rewarding to get to the top of the mountain and share your experience with others than to show up by yourself, exhausted.

—Shandel Slaten, executive coach

Teams share the burden and divide the grief.

—Doug Smith, author and team-building expert

———⟶◆⟵———

Gettin' good players is easy. Gettin' 'em to play together is the hard part.

—Casey Stengel, baseball legend

———⟶◆⟵———

Unity is strength. . . . When there is teamwork and collaboration, wonderful things can be achieved.

—Mattie Stepanek, poet

When you hand good people possibility, they do great things.

—Biz Stone, cofounder of Twitter

───◆◆◆───

A boat doesn't go forward if each one is rowing [his] own way.

—Swahili proverb

───◆◆◆───

It is amazing how much people can get done if they do not worry about who gets the credit.

—Sandra Swinney, author

Teamwork is so important that it is virtually impossible for you to reach the heights of your capabilities or make the money that you want without becoming very good at it.

—Brian Tracy, author

Overcoming barriers to performance is how groups become teams.

—Unknown

Good company in a journey makes the way seem shorter.

—Izaak Walton, English writer

If you don't kick things around with people, you are out of it. Nobody, I always say, can be anybody without somebody being around.

—John Wheeler, theoretical physicist

Creating a better world requires teamwork, partnerships, and collaboration, as we need an entire army of companies to work together to build a better world within the next few decades. This means corporations must embrace the benefits of cooperating with one another.

—Simon Mainwaring, branding consultant, advertising creative director, and social media expert

Keep in touch with people you didn't hire but you really liked; you never know when you might need to call upon them to help you out.

—Melinda Emerson, founder and CEO of Quintessence Multimedia

He who has learned to disagree without being disagreeable has discovered the most valuable secret of a diplomat.

—Robert Estabrook, journalist

Everyone should be respected as an individual, but no one idolized.

—Albert Einstein, developer of the theory of relativity

Individuals don't win; teams do. Wal-Mart is just a spectacular example of what happens when people find a way to work together—where almost four hundred thousand people have come together as a group like this, with a real feeling of partnership, and have been able, for the most part, to put the needs of their individual egos behind the needs of their team.

—Sam Walton, founder of Wal-Mart

Vision and Goals

When editor John Clarke included the idiom "seeing is believing" in an anthology of proverbs in 1639, he could not have realized that several centuries later it would be the perfect definition of *vision,* as the word is meant in the business world. For any newly minted businessperson, one of the most important factors for success is the ability to conjure a mental image of it by some future date. Vision helps the businessperson identify and set goals, and it forces him to focus. Visions are as varied as the universe of business. By communicating the vision to colleagues, the businessperson leads his entire team toward its fulfillment. The quotes here highlight the importance of having a vision—and goals—and the perils inherent in setting out without one.

Confusion of goals and perfection of means seems, in my opinion, to characterize our age.

—Albert Einstein, developer of the theory of relativity

———◆———

If you want to be happy, set a goal that commands your thoughts, liberates your energy, and inspires your hopes.

—Andrew Carnegie, steel industrialist

———◆———

If you have more than three priorities, you don't have any.

—Jim Collins, business consultant, author, and lecturer (from his book *Good to Great: Why Some Companies Make the Leap . . . and Others Don't,* 2001)

An entrepreneur must pitch a potential investor for what the company is worth as well as sell the dream on how much of a profit can be made.

—Daymond John, entrepreneur and CEO of FUBU

—◆—

Your long-term goals should be realistic, challenging, and attainable statements of where you want your company to be in three to five years following the direction outlined in your mission statement. Long-term goals function as starting and organizational points, to make it easier to process, prioritize, allocate resources, and coordinate related short-term goals and objectives.

—Peter J. Patsula, founder of Patsula Media and author

—◆—

To accomplish great things, we must not only act but also dream, not only plan but also believe.

—Anatole France, poet and journalist

A visionary company doesn't simply balance between idealism and profitability: it seeks to be highly idealistic and highly profitable. A visionary company doesn't simply balance between preserving a tightly held core ideology and stimulating vigorous change and movement; it does both to an extreme.

—Jim Collins, business consultant, author, and lecturer

I present a dream. They are worlds you would like to be a part of. In that world, you'd wear that kind of thing. I see a whole feeling. I don't see a pant. Everything is connected to something else. Nothing is apart. I design into living. It's a lifestyle.

—Ralph Lauren, fashion designer

The best vision is insight.

—Malcolm S. Forbes, publisher of *Forbes* magazine

Set your goals, then develop an actionable plan to make them a reality. Then, don't forget about those goals. Keep them front and center to everything you do.

—Jayson Demers, entrepreneur and columnist (from *Entrepreneur* magazine, August 11, 2014)

I am sure I'd have made a better all-around man if I hadn't lost so much time just making a living.

—Herbert Hoover, US president

The secret to productive goal setting is in establishing clearly defined goals, writing them down and then focusing on them several times a day with words, pictures and emotions as if we've already achieved them.

—Denis Waitley, motivational speaker, writer, and consultant

Capital isn't scarce; vision is.

—Sam Walton, founder of Wal-Mart

Inventing your dream is the first and biggest step toward making it come true.

—Biz Stone, cofounder of Twitter

To turn really interesting ideas and fledgling technologies into a company that can continue to innovate for years, it requires a lot of disciplines.

—Steve Jobs, cofounder of Apple and Pixar Animation

I'd encourage [you] to think big and be delusional when setting goals. Yes, delusional. The biggest mistake that I made with my first business was I didn't think big enough. I limited my success by just focusing on a small geographic area and focusing on hitting small sales targets. Now when I set my goals, I make sure that they are ridiculous. I prefer to work extremely hard and fall short on my ridiculous goals than to achieve mediocre goals.

—Warren Cassell Jr., Caribbean entrepreneur

All successful people—men and women—are big dreamers. They imagine what their future could be, ideal in every respect, and then they work every day toward their distant vision, that goal or purpose.

—Brian Tracy, author

If you are not making the progress that you would like to make and are capable of making, it is simply because your goals are not clearly defined.

—Paul J. Meyer, founder of Success Motivation Institute

The two most important days in your life are the day you are born and the day you find out why.

—Mark Twain, author and humorist

If you have a goal, if you want to be successful, if you really want to do it and become another Estée Lauder, you've got to work hard, you've got to stick to it and you've got to believe in what you're doing.

—Estée Lauder, cofounder of Estée Lauder Companies

A goal is a dream with a deadline.

—Napoleon Hill, pioneer of the modern genre of personal success

You don't have to be a genius or a visionary or even a college graduate to be successful. You just need a framework and a dream.

—Michael Dell, founder of Dell Computer

Developing the plan is actually laying out the sequence of events that have to occur for you to achieve your goal.

—George L. Morrisey, author

The rule of my life is to make business a pleasure, and pleasure my business.

—Aaron Burr, US Vice President

Savvy entrepreneurs adopting an abundance mindset realize there's enough business to go around. The next time you're networking, consider approaching someone you think is a competitor. Explore the possibilities of referring business to them.

 —Lisa A. Mininni, author

Cherish your visions and your dreams as they are the children of your soul, the blueprints of your ultimate achievements.

 —Napoleon Hill, pioneer of the modern genre of personal success

Business, more than any other occupation, is a continual dealing with the future; it is a continual calculation, an instinctive exercise in foresight.

 —Henry R. Luce, founder of *Time* magazine

Nothing is more terrible than activity without insight.

   —Thomas Carlyle, Scottish philosopher, essayist, satirist, and historian

———

Most of today's market leaders are those companies who had the foresight to recognize the changing landscape in today's modern business world. The new business "battle ground" has been very cruel to those companies that have fallen behind the information curve.

   —Futurevisionweb.com

———

Someone is sitting in the shade today because someone planted a tree a long time ago.

   —Warren Buffett, legendary investor and CEO of Berkshire Hathaway

Vision is the art of seeing things invisible.

—Jonathan Swift, Anglo-Irish satirist, essayist, political
pamphleteer, poet, and cleric

We wanted Nike to be the world's best sports and fit-
ness company. Once you say that, you have a focus. You
don't end up making wing tips or sponsoring the next
Rolling Stones world tour.

—Phil Knight, founder of Nike

A man to carry on a successful business must have imagination. He must see things as in a vision, a dream of the
whole thing.

—Charles M. Schwab, steel magnate

Companies succeed because they are . . . value driven. Excellent companies believe that the basic philosophy of an organization has far more to do with its achievements than do technological or economic resources, organizational structures and innovation. In other words, companies succeed if its members share a common vision of their future, feel they are important part of the whole, and look out for each other.

—Peter J. Patsula, founder of Patsula Media and author

Great lives are the culmination of great thoughts followed by great actions.

—Peter Sinclair, author

The entrepreneur is essentially a visualizer and actualizer. . . . He can visualize something, and when he visualizes it he sees exactly how to make it happen.

—Robert L. Schwartz, author and Harvard professor emeritus

What the mind of man can conceive and believe, it can achieve.

    —Napoleon Hill, pioneer of the modern genre of personal success

There is no top. There are always further heights to reach.

    —Jascha Heifetz, virtuoso violinist

The more you dream, the farther you get.

    —Michael Phelps, Olympic gold medalist

A person who aims at nothing is sure to hit it.
　　　—Unknown

News Corporation, today, reaches people at home and at work . . . when they're thinking . . . when they're laughing . . . and when they are making choices that have enormous impact. The unique potential and duty of a media company are to help its audiences connect to the issues that define our time.
　　　—Rupert Murdoch, media mogul

If your only goal is to become rich, you will never achieve it.
　　　—John D. Rockefeller, industrialist, cofounder of
　　　Standard Oil Co., and philanthropist

Globalization has changed us into a company that searches the world, not just to sell or to source, but to find intellectual capital—the world's best talents and greatest ideas.

—Jack Welch, chairman and CEO of GE

Decision Making

Of all the complex variables that go into building a successful business, sound decision making may be the most vital. Wharton's executive education curriculum includes "The Strategic Decision-Making Mindset," and first-year MBA students at Stanford are required to take "Data Analysis and Decision Making." The quotes here are a compilation of decision-making best practices. Above all, they extol the value of honest and timely decision making.

I never get the accountants in before I start up a business. It's done on gut feeling, especially if I can see that they are taking the mickey out of the consumer.

—Sir Richard Branson, billionaire entrepreneur and founder of Virgin Airlines

———◆———

Making good decisions is a crucial skill at every level.

—Peter F. Drucker, management consultant, educator, and author

———◆———

A decision is only as strong as the belief standing behind it.

—Isaiah Hankel, author and speaker

You can't build a strong corporation with a lot of com-
mittees and a Board that has to be consulted at every
turn. You have to be able to make decisions on your
own.

— Rupert Murdoch, media mogul

⸺◆⸺

In a start-up company, you basically throw out all
assumptions every three weeks.

— William Lyon Phelps, author, critic, and scholar

⸺◆⸺

We are always waiting for the perfect brief from the perfect client. It almost never happens. . . . Whatever is on
your desk right now, that's the one. Make it the best you
possibly can.

— Paul Arden, advertising executive

Before you start some work, always ask yourself three questions—Why am I doing it, What the results might be and Will I be successful? Only when you think deeply and find satisfactory answers to these questions, go ahead.

> —Chanakya, Indian teacher, philosopher, royal advisor, economist, and jurist

Follow effective actions with quiet reflection. From the quiet reflection will come even more effective action.

> —Peter F. Drucker, management consultant, educator, and author

Nothing you are choosing to do for yourself is worth the tears and feelings of dread every single morning. NOTHING.

> —Mary Mihalic, author

Have a very good reason for everything you do.

—Laurence Olivier, actor

————◆◆————

You must either modify your dreams or magnify your skills.

—Jim Rohn, entrepreneur, author, and motivational speaker

————◆◆————

There's always chaos and there are always unknowns. Just do the best you can with what's in front of you and go.

—Nicholas Thompson, editor of NewYorker.com

If you are a consistent moneymaker, you will be a good decision-maker. Sometimes the window of opportunity is open only briefly. Waiting isn't a decision, although many people think it is.

—T. Boone Pickens, Texas oilman and investor

Whenever you see a successful business, someone once made a courageous decision.

—Peter F. Drucker, management consultant, educator, and author

It often requires more courage to dare to do right than to fear to do wrong.

—Abraham Lincoln, US president

Being trustworthy requires: Doing the right thing. And doing things right.

—Don Peppers, founding partner of management consultant Peppers & Rogers Group

It is our choices that show what we truly are, far more than our abilities.

—J. K. Rowling, *Harry Potter* author

One's philosophy is not best expressed in words; it is expressed in the choices one makes . . . and the choices we make are ultimately our responsibility.

—Eleanor Roosevelt, US first lady

To think is easy. To act is difficult. To act as one thinks
is the most difficult.

    ——Johann Wolfgang von Goethe, German writer and
      statesman

Motivation

Businesses generally can't function without employees. But few workers are entirely self-motivated to perform at their full potential. And an unmotivated workforce can dim the prospects of a business. Turnover is likely to be troublesome, and the quality of work far from stellar. Consequently, a manager's motivational talents carry a premium. These leaders are responsible for knowing the various motivational buttons that spur her workforce to superior results. Is it money that stimulates a particular employee to perform at his highest level? Or do rewards or recognition induce an employee to be her best? Surely, inspiring words are effective motivational tools. And businesspeople have to learn to motivate themselves—and stay motivated. Make space in the toolbox for the quotes below.

If you have time to whine then you have time to find a solution.

> —Dee Dee Artner, author and behavioral expert (from her book *Positivity Now: How Simple Steps Can Help You Work Effectively, Communicate Positively and Live Successfully!*, 2014)

If we try and fail, we have temporary disappointments. But if we do not try at all, we have permanent regrets.

> —Bern Williams, English moral philosopher

Motivation is a fire from within. If someone else tries to light that fire under you, chances are it will burn very briefly.

> —Stephen R. Covey, educator, author, and businessman

Make the most of what you have. I operated, full time, on that precept. If you can't have everything you think you deserve at that moment, you would do well to surround yourself with symbols of your ideals. In that small office, I surrounded myself with touches of the good life, the lovely and intricately tapestried life of my imagination, an imagination that has always been, I'm proud to say, large enough to admit any possibility.

—Estée Lauder, cofounder of Estée Lauder Companies

Everything you want is on the other side of fear.

—Jack Canfield, author and entrepreneur

The only lifelong, reliable motivations are those that come from within, and one of the strongest of those is the joy and pride that grow from knowing that you've just done something as well as you can do it.

—Lloyd Dobens and Clare Crawford-Mason, coauthors of *Thinking About Quality*

Creating awareness about what motivates us gives us the greater knowledge to choose.

—Lisa A. Mininni, author

There's always the motivation of wanting to win. Everybody has that. But a champion needs, in his attitude, a motivation above and beyond winning.

—Pat Riley, professional basketball coach and executive

Why climb the corporate ladder when you can build an elevator in your own building?

—Joshua E. Leyenhorst, owner of Promadim Promotional Products, British Columbia

We know nothing about motivation. All we can do is write books about it.

—Peter F. Drucker, management consultant, educator, and author

——◆——

Every moment is a fresh beginning.

—T. S. Eliot, author

——◆——

The will to win, the desire to succeed, the urge to reach your full potential . . . these are the keys that will unlock the door to personal excellence.

—Confucius, Chinese philosopher

Great spirits have always encountered violent opposition from mediocre minds.

—Albert Einstein, developer of the theory of relativity

———◆———

Management is nothing more than motivating other people.

—Lee Iacocca, chairman and CEO of Chrysler Motors

———◆———

The primary motivation wasn't making money, but making an impact.

—Sean Parker, cofounder of Facebook

Motivation is simple. You eliminate those who are not motivated.

—Lou Holtz, legendary college basketball coach

My only real motivation is not to be hassled—that, and the fear of losing my job. But you know, Bob, that will only make someone work just hard enough not to get fired.

—Peter Gibbons, character in the movie *Office Space*

The whole idea of motivation is a trap. Forget motivation. Just do it. Exercise, lose weight, test your blood sugar, or whatever. Do it without motivation. And then, guess what? After you start doing the thing, that's when the motivation comes and makes it easy for you to keep on doing it.

—John C. Maxwell, author, speaker, and pastor

The only way to get people to like working hard is to motivate them. Today, people must understand why they're working hard. Every individual in an organization is motivated by something different.

—Rick Pitino, college basketball coach

❦

Get mocked at for as much as you can, fail as much as you can but don't quit. Let every mockery, every failure, be a source of inspiration for you to reach for greatness and that greatness will silence your critics.

—Ajaero Tony Martins, Nigerian entrepreneur
and investor

❦

People often say that motivation doesn't last. Well, neither does bathing—that's why we recommend it daily.

—Zig Ziglar, motivational speaker

Every accomplishment starts with a decision to try.
—Unknown

———◆———

Amateurs sit and wait for inspiration, the rest of us just get up and go to work.
—Stephen King, author

———◆———

Those who seize the day become seriously rich.
—Richard Koch, British author, speaker, and investor

Nobody motivates today's workers. If it doesn't come from within, it doesn't come. Fun helps remove the barriers that allow people to motivate themselves.

—Herman Cain, Republican presidential aspirant

You don't have to be great to start, but you do have to start to be great.

—Unknown

It is easier to do a job right than to explain why you didn't.

—Martin Van Buren, US president

When you look at people who are successful, you will find that they aren't the people who are motivated, but have consistency in their motivation.

—Arsene Wenger, French football manager and former player

If in your mind's eye you see a successful venture, a deal made, a profit accomplished, it has a superb chance of actually happening. Projecting your mind into a successful situation is the most powerful means to achieve goals. If you spent time with pictures of failure in your mind, you will orchestrate failure.

—Estée Lauder, cofounder of Estée Lauder Companies

Investing

The business world features at least two forms of investing: the business of investing, which is associated with Wall Street and stock trading, and business investing. The latter typically entails sinking profits back into the company to finance further development of the business. The quotes below cover both forms, and reflect the wisdom of some of the investment world's most astute investors and investment analysts, among others.

A market is the combined behavior of thousands of people responding to information, misinformation and whim.

—Kenneth Chang, *New York Times* journalist

❖

No one was ever ruined by taking a profit.

—Stock exchange maxim

❖

Never make an investment transaction that hinges upon selling your home or taking out a mortgage on your home. This is a proven recipe for disaster.

—Tom Ajamie and Bruce Kelly, co-authors of *Financial Serial Killers: Inside the World of Wall Street Money Hustlers, Swindlers, and Con Men*

When somebody buys a stock it's because they think it's going to go up and the person who sold it to them thinks it's going to go down. Somebody's wrong.

—George Ross, Trump Organization executive

———◆———

The key to making money is to stay invested.

—Suze Orman, personal finance expert

———◆———

I cannot understand why an investor . . . elects to put money into a business that is his 20th favorite rather than simply adding that money to his top choices—the businesses he understands best and that present the least risk, along with the greatest profit potential. In the words of the prophet Mae West: "Too much of a good thing can be wonderful."

—Warren Buffett, legendary investor and CEO of Berkshire Hathaway (from his letter to Berkshire Hathaway shareholders, 1994)

Running the company for the shareholders often reduces its long-term growth potential.

—Ha-Joon Chang, South Korean economist

I think you have to learn that there's a company behind every stock, and that there's only one real reason why stocks go up. Companies go from doing poorly to doing well or small companies grow to large companies.

—Peter Lynch, Fidelity Fund manager

In confusing stock options with ownership, corporations confuse trappings with substance.

—James Surowiecki, journalist (from *The New Yorker* magazine, November 9, 2009)

When buying shares, ask yourself, would you buy the whole company?

—Rene Rivkin, Australian entrepreneur, investor, and
investment advisor

Do your own investigation into a company before investing in it. Don't rely on the media or stock analysts since they have their own agendas.

—Tom Ajamie and Bruce Kelly, co-authors of *Financial*
Serial Killers: Inside the World of Wall Street Money
Hustlers, Swindlers, and Con Men

If it was my business, I wouldn't talk about it. It is very vulgar to talk about one's business. Only people like stockbrokers do that, and then merely at dinner parties.

—Oscar Wilde, Irish playwright, novelist, essayist,
and poet

Experience taught me a few things. One is to listen to your gut, no matter how good something sounds on paper. The second is that you're generally better off sticking with what you know. And the third is that sometimes your best investments are the ones you don't make.

—Donald Trump, real estate developer, author, and presidential candidate

---

Above all else, in other words, the stock market is people. It is people trying to read the future. And it is this intensely human quality that makes the stock market so dramatic an arena in which men and women pit their conflicting judgments, their hopes and fears, strengths and weaknesses, greed and ideals.

—Bernard Baruch, financier, stock investor, philanthropist, and statesman

---

It's far better to buy a wonderful company at a fair price than a fair company at a wonderful price.

—Warren Buffett, legendary investor and CEO of Berkshire Hathaway

I have a problem with too much money. I can't reinvest it fast enough, and because I reinvest it, more money comes in. Yes, the rich do get richer.

—Robert Kiyosaki, entrepreneur and author

———◆———

I invested in many companies, and I'm happy this one worked. This is capitalism. You invest in stock, it goes up, it goes down. You know, if you don't like capitalism, you don't like making money with stock, move to Cuba or China.

—Terry McAuliffe, governor of Virginia

———◆———

The real key to making money in stocks is not to get scared out of them.

—Peter Lynch, Fidelity Fund manager

Making money, it seems, is all about the velocity of moving it around, so that it can exist in Hong Kong one moment and Wall Street a split second later.

—Richard Dooling, novelist and screenwriter

To get rich, you have to be making money while you're asleep.

—David Bailey, artist (from interview in British newspaper *The Independent*, March 2, 1998)

A lot of people love Oreos. So their manufacturer is making money. That means more dividends for shareholders.

—Maria Bartiromo, business television anchor

Millionaires don't play the blame game but the gain game.

—Dee Dee Artner, author and behavioral expert

◆

Before you can really start setting financial goals, you need to determine where you stand financially.

—David Bach, financial consultant

◆

Talent can be hired, money has to be earned.

— Vishnu, Hindu male deity

Only buy something that you'd be perfectly happy to hold if the market shut down for ten years.

— Warren Buffett, legendary investor and CEO of Berkshire Hathaway

———◆———

If you change the rules of the market, you can be more successful than your competitors.

— Max McKeown, English writer and consultant

———◆———

The more you delay the process of extracting value from your network and channels, the faster you will build audience and good will. Then good will and value can be extracted more efficiently later on, when it matters.

— Chris Brogan and Julien Smith (from their coauthored book *The Impact Equation: Are You Making Things Happen or Just Making Noise?*, 2012)

Today people who hold cash equivalents feel comfortable. They shouldn't. They have opted for a terrible long-term asset, one that pays virtually nothing and is certain to depreciate in value.

> —Warren Buffett, legendary investor and CEO of Berkshire Hathaway

Making money from enforcing patents is no more wrong than investing in preferred stock.

> —Nathan Myhrvold, Silicon Valley entrepreneur and investor

Character

What type of personality works best in the business world? What type works best with business teams? How can business people reconcile their personalities with their corporations? Employees need self-knowledge and self-confidence to succeed in today's workplace. By figuring out who they are and how they affect others, they can stay true to themselves and contribute more to—and get more from—the world of business.

In an ideal world, managers would constantly be thinking about how to best utilize their people—and clients would always unearth your greatest potential. Unfortunately, the reality is that bosses and clients are as worried about their own careers as you are about your own. You must take the task of marketing your strengths into your own hands.

—Scott Belsky, entrepreneur and author (from his book *Making Ideas Happen: Overcoming the Obstacles between Vision and Reality,* 2010)

We simply attempt to be fearful when others are greedy and to be greedy when others are fearful.

—Warren Buffett, legendary investor and chairman of Berkshire Hathaway

---

To sin by silence when they should protest makes cowards of men.

—Abraham Lincoln, US president

If a man will begin with certainties he shall end in doubts; but if he will be content to begin with doubts he shall end in certainties.

    —Francis Bacon, English philosopher, statesman, scientist, jurist, orator, and author

For many of us in this room today, let's start out by admitting we're lucky. We don't live in the world our mothers lived in, our grandmothers lived in, where career choices for women were so limited.

    —Sheryl Sandberg, chief operating officer of Facebook

Education begins the gentleman, but reading, good company and reflection must finish him.

    —John Locke, English philosopher and physician

Believe in yourself! Have faith in your abilities! Without a humble but reasonable confidence in your own powers you cannot be successful or happy.

—Norman Vincent Peale, minister, author, and a pioneer of "positive thinking"

If you are filled with pride, then you will have no room for wisdom.

—African proverb

Be patient with yourself. Self-growth is tender; it's holy ground. There's no greater investment.

—Steven Covey, educator, author, and businessman

Watch your manner of speech if you wish to develop a peaceful state of mind. Start each day by affirming peaceful, contented and happy attitudes and your days will tend to be pleasant and successful.

—Norman Vincent Peale, minister, author, and a pioneer of "positive thinking"

Chance favors only the prepared mind.

—Louis Pasteur, chemist and investor of pasteurization

I had to get into a place for myself of thinking what I would create for myself if I didn't have to worry about making money.

—Jada Pinkett Smith, actress

467

Think twice before you speak, because your words and influence will plant the seed of either success or failure in the mind of another.

> —Napoleon Hill, pioneer of the modern genre of personal success

The important thing is that you work for yourself, not for my approval. Not for my praise. But that you come to feel that doing well matters to you, and you become your most loyal fan, as well as your most severe critic.

> —as told to Judith Rodin, president at the Rockefeller Foundation, by her first-grade teacher, Miss Invernessy

The quality of a person's life is in direct proportion to their commitment to excellence, regardless of their chosen field of endeavor.

> —Vince Lombardi, professional football coaching legend

Find out who you are and be that person. That's what your soul was put on this Earth to be. Find that truth, live that truth and everything else will come.

— Ellen DeGeneres, talk show host and actress

———◆———

Life's challenges are not supposed to paralyze you; they're supposed to help you discover who you are.

— Bernice Johnson Reagon, singer

———◆———

Always remember, you have within you the strength, the patience, and the passion to reach for the stars to change the world.

— Harriet Tubman, abolitionist

Few are those who see with their own eyes and feel with their own hearts.

—Albert Einstein, developer of the theory of relativity

No man ever got very high by pulling other people down. The intelligent merchant does not knock his competitors. The sensible worker does not work those who work with him. Don't knock your friends. Don't knock your enemies. Don't knock yourself.

—Alfred Lord Tennyson, poet laureate of Great Britain and Ireland

If you don't value your time, neither will others. Stop giving away your time and talents. Value what you know and start charging for it.

—Kim Garst, founder and CEO of Boom! Social

Don't take too much advice. Most people who have a lot of advice to give—with a few exceptions—generalize whatever they did. Don't overanalyze everything. I myself have been guilty of overthinking problems. Just build things and find out if they work.

—Ben Silbermann, founder of Pinterest

———◆◆◆———

We must accept finite disappointment, but never lose infinite hope.

—Martin Luther King Jr., civil rights leader

———◆◆◆———

You can't stop negative thoughts from coming in, but you can make sure they leave as quickly as they enter.

—Nkem Paul, author

471

You must do the things you think you cannot do.
—Eleanor Roosevelt, US first lady

Keep away from people who belittle your ambitions. Small people always do that, but the really great make you feel that you, too, can become great.
—Mark Twain, author and humorist

Setting an example is not the main means of influencing others; it is the only means.
—Albert Einstein, developer of the theory of relativity

If a man lives his life to himself and has no regard for humanity he will be the most miserable man on earth. All the money he can get will not help him to forget his discontent. To hide one's self from the world and live alone, secluded from one's fellow men like a hermit, will make a man's nature sullen and wretched.

—John D. Rockefeller, industrialist, cofounder of Standard Oil Co., and philanthropist

You are in control of your priorities—you can erase old priorities and define new priorities at will.

—Isaiah Hankel, author and speaker

What is the point of being alive if you don't at least try to do something remarkable?

—John Green, author

473

The potential of controlling and living a successful life according to your terms depends on how you think. Your perception is your world. You can create the life you want and in fact, you can even shape the way you want it.

—Dee Dee Artner, author and behavioral expert

Keep calm. The market is going to be open every day. Know who you are, so if a broker calls you and says, "If you don't do this right now, you're going to miss it," be willing to miss it.

—Tom Ajamie and Bruce Kelly, coauthors of *Financial Serial Killers: Inside the World of Wall Street Money Hustlers, Swindlers, and Con Men*

Associate yourself with men of good quality if you esteem your own reputation; for 'tis better to be alone than in bad company.

—George Washington, US president

Things work out best for those who make the best of how things work out.

—John Wooden, legendary UCLA basketball coach

❖

Few people are capable of expressing with equanimity opinions which differ from the prejudices of their social environment. Most people are even incapable of forming such opinions.

—Albert Einstein, developer of the general theory of relativity

❖

If we were all content with the way our fathers and mothers believed, then we would not progress at all, and thinking and reasoning would become unfashionable.

—King Gillette, founder of Gillette Safety Razor Co.

Whatever task you undertake, do it with all your heart and soul. Always be courteous, never be discouraged. Beware of him who promises something for nothing. Do not blame anybody for your mistakes and failures. Do not look for approval except the consciousness of doing your best.

    —Bernard Baruch, financier, stock investor, philanthropist, and statesman

⊷◆⊶

Your time is limited, so don't waste it living someone else's life. Don't be trapped by dogma— which is living with the results of other people's thinking. Don't let the noise of other's opinions drown out your own inner voice. And most important, have the courage to follow your heart and intuition. They somehow already know what you truly want to become. Everything else is secondary.

    —Steve Jobs, cofounder of Apple and Pixar Animation

As a child I felt myself to be alone, and I am still, because I know things and must hint at things which others apparently know nothing of, and for the most part do not want to know.

—Carl Gustav Jung, Swiss psychologist and lead author of *Memories, Dreams, Reflections*

Well, they perhaps tend to think I've not got as thick a skin as I have. You know, I don't mind what people say about me. I've never read a book about myself.

—Rupert Murdoch, media mogul (*Fortune* magazine, April 10, 2014)

It gives me great pleasure indeed to see the stubbornness of an incorrigible nonconformist warmly acclaimed.

—Albert Einstein, developer of the general theory of relativity

A life lived with integrity—even if it lacks the trappings of fame and fortune—is a shining star in whose light others may follow in the years to come.

—Denis Waitley, motivational speaker, writer, and consultant

———

I've always thought that each person invented himself . . . for whatever reason, through whatever circumstance, through whatever he is gone through . . . that we are each a figment of our own imagination. . . . And some people have a greater ability to imagine than others.

—David Geffen, entertainment mogul (from YouTube video, November 6, 2013)

———

He who joyfully marches to music in rank and file has already earned my contempt. He has been given a large brain by mistake, since for him the spinal cord would suffice.

—Albert Einstein, developer of the general theory of relativity

If you accept the expectations of others, especially negative ones, then you never will change the outcome.
—Michael Jordan, NBA legend

One man with courage makes a majority.
—Andrew Jackson, US president

I believe that one defines oneself by reinvention. To not be like your parents. To not be like your friends. To be yourself. You cut yourself out of stone.
—Henry Rollins, musician, actor, television and radio host, and comedian

You can spend minutes, hours, days, weeks, or even months overanalyzing a situation; trying to put the pieces together, justifying what could've, would've happened. . . . Or you can just leave the pieces on the floor and move the fuck on.

—Tupac Shakur, rap music star

———◆———

The trouble is that you think you have time.

—Jack Kornfield, author and teacher

———◆———

Procrastination is one of the most common and deadliest of diseases and its toll on success and happiness is heavy.

—Dr. Wayne W. Dyer, philosopher, self-help author, and motivational speaker

The only thing holding you back is you. Commit to developing the mindset of a winner, set your goals and chase them down. Remember, a dog in the hunt ain't got no fleas!

—Andy Albright, author

***

Finish each day and be done with it. You have done what you could. Some blunders and absurdities no doubt crept in; forget them as soon as you can. Tomorrow is a new day. You shall begin it serenely and with too high a spirit to be encumbered with your old nonsense.

—Ralph Waldo Emerson, philosopher, poet, and essayist

***

Whenever you are asked if you can do a job, tell 'em, "Certainly I can!" Then get busy and find out how to do it.

—Theodore Roosevelt, US president

Let us not be content to wait and see what will happen, but give us the determination to make the right things happen.

—Peter Marshall, author

We should take care not to make the intellect our god; it has, of course, powerful muscles, but no personality.

—Albert Einstein, developer of the theory of relativity

If you close your eyes to facts, you will learn through accidents.

—African proverb

For all of its faults (capitalism), it gives most hardworking people a chance to improve themselves economically, even as the deck is stacked in favor of the privileged few. Here are the choices most of us face in such a system: Get bitter or get busy.

—Bill O'Reilly, television host, author, journalist, and a political commentator

He who has relied least on fortune is established the strongest.

—Machiavelli, Italian Renaissance political philosopher

All my life, people have said that I wasn't going to make it.

—Ted Turner, founder of CNN and Turner Broadcasting

Life isn't worth living unless you're willing to take some big chances and go for broke.

> —Eliot Wigginton, oral historian, folklorist, writer, and educator

Any man worth his salt will stick up for what he believes right, but it takes a slightly better man to acknowledge instantly and without reservation that he is in error.

> —Andrew Jackson, US president

Please think about your legacy, because you're writing it every day.

> —Gary Vaynerchuk, entrepreneur, investor, author, and Internet personality

God gives every bird a worm, but he does not throw it into the nest.
—Swedish proverb

I didn't think of discouragement. What I thought of was getting that job.
—John D. Rockefeller, industrial, cofounder of Standard Oil Co., and philanthropist

To the degree we're not living our dreams, our comfort zone has more control of us than we have over ourselves.
—Peter McWilliams, self-help author and marijuana legalization advocate

Our business in life is not to get ahead of others, but to get ahead of ourselves—to break our own records, to outstrip our yesterday by our today.

—Stewart B. Johnson, artist

———◆———

Some people want it to happen, some wish it would happen, others make it happen.

—Michael Jordan, NBA legend

———◆———

You become what you think about.

—Napoleon Hill, pioneer of the modern genre of personal success

Do not worry about your difficulties in mathematics. I can assure you mine are still greater.

    —Albert Einstein, developer of the general theory of relativity

———◆———

Optimism is the faith that leads to achievement. Nothing can be done without hope and confidence.

    —Helen Keller, author, journalist and activist for the blind

———◆———

Confidence is knowing that you can walk into any situation with the skills, strengths, and abilities you need.

    —Marci G. Fox, psychologist

Every person is special! I sincerely believe this. Each of us wants to feel good about himself or herself, but to me it is just as important to make others feel the same way. Whenever I meet someone, I try to imagine him wearing an invisible sign that says: Make Me Feel Important! I respond to this sign immediately, and it works wonders.

—Mary Kay Ash, founder of Mary Kay Cosmetics

You can close more business in two months by becoming interested in other people than you can in two years by trying to get people interested in you.

—Dale Carnegie, writer, lecturer, and developer of self-improvement courses (from his book *How to Win Friends and Influence People,* 1936)

Action is a great restorer and builder of confidence. Inaction is not only the result, but the cause, of fear. Perhaps the action you take will be successful; perhaps different action or adjustments will have to follow. But any action is better than no action at all.

—Norman Vincent Peale, minister, author, and a pioneer of "positive thinking"

We are what we repeatedly do. Excellence, then, is not an act, but a habit.

—Aristotle, Greek philosopher

What we truly need to do is often what we most feel like avoiding.

—David Allen, author

If you are a winner by the judgments of few judges and not by your performance, you are not a real winner.

—Amit Kalantri, author

If you're going to invent new things you've also got to be able—this goes along with long-term orientation, you've got to be able to endure a lot of criticism.

—Jeff Bezos, founder of Amazon.com

<hr>

We always overestimate the change that will occur in the next two years and underestimate the change that will occur in the next ten. Don't let yourself be lulled into inaction.

—Bill Gates, cofounder of Microsoft and philanthropist

<hr>

Men who are resolved to find a way for themselves will always find opportunities enough; and if they do not find them, they will make them.

—Samuel Smiles, Scottish author and political reformer

I have a plan, and I'm following it. I can focus on doing what is within my control, and I don't need to be afraid of the results.

—Elizabeth Grace Saunders, time-management coach

In trying to find who you are, be less destructive and more constructive. Look at art or whatever your passion is and be productive.

—Nirrimi Joy Hakanson, fashion photographer

God helps them that help themselves.

—Benjamin Franklin, US founding father and inventor

Quality begins on the inside . . . and then works its way out.

    —Bob Moawad, author

It makes no sense to worry about things you have no control over because there's nothing you can do about them, and why worry about things you do control? The activity of worrying keeps you immobilized.

    —Dr. Wayne W. Dyer, philosopher, self-help author,
      and motivational speaker

Everyone who's ever taken a shower has an idea. It's the person who gets out of the shower, dries off and does something about it who makes a difference.

    —Nolan Bushnell, engineer and founder of Atari Inc.
      and Chuck E. Cheese's Pizza-Time Theaters chain

If you don't know where you're going, you'll end up somewhere else.
—David Campbell, author

———◆———

If you don't make things happen then things will happen to you.
—Robert Collier, self-help author

———◆———

The sleeping fox catches no poultry.
—Benjamin Franklin, US founding father and inventor

The potential of controlling and living a successful life according to your terms depends on how you think. Your perception is your world. You can create the life you want and in fact, you can even shape the way you want it.

—Dee Dee Artner, author and behavioral expert

I don't want to be in a position where I'm playing roles I'm comfortable with and making money, but doing it without feeling like I'm growing.

—Rodrigo Santoro, Brazilian actor

Belief in oneself is one of the most important bricks in building any successful venture.

—Lydia M. Child, abolitionist, women's rights activist, novelist, and journalist

People have within their own hands the tools to fashion their own destiny.

—Murray D. Lincoln, founder of the Nationwide Insurance Companies

None of us, including me, ever do great things. But we can all do small things, with great love, and together we can do something wonderful.

—Mother Theresa, Roman Catholic nun and missionary

Always bear in mind that your own resolution to success is more important than any other one thing.

—Abraham Lincoln, US president

You must expect great things of yourself before you can do them.

—Michael Jordan, NBA legend

———◆———

[A]ll too often, a successful new business model becomes the business model for companies not creative enough to invent their own.

—Gary Hamel, management expert

———◆———

If you want to be truly successful invest in yourself to get the knowledge you need to find your unique factor. When you find it and focus on it and persevere your success will blossom.

—Sydney Madwed, public speaker, poet, lyricist, and author

You were born to win, but to be a winner, you must plan to win, prepare to win, and expect to win.

—Zig Ziglar, motivational speaker

You are where you are and what you are because of yourself, nothing else. Nature is neutral. Nature doesn't care. If you do what other successful people do, you will enjoy the same results and rewards that they do. And if you don't, you won't.

—Brian Tracy, author

People become really quite remarkable when they start thinking that they can do things. When they believe in themselves, they have the first secret of success.

—Norman Vincent Peale, minister, author, and a pioneer of "positive thinking"

Trust your instincts, know what you want, and believe in your ability to achieve it.

—Biz Stone, cofounder of Twitter

Will power is the key to success. Successful people strive no matter what they feel by applying their will to overcome apathy, doubt or fear.

—Dan Millman, author and personal development lecturer

The best way to not feel hopeless is to get up and do something. Don't wait for good things to happen to you. If you go out and make some good things happen, you will fill the world with hope, you will fill yourself with hope.

—Barack Obama, US president

⟨⟩

You have brains in your head. You have feet in your shoes. You can steer yourself, any direction you choose.

—Dr. Seuss, children's author (from his book *Oh, The Places You'll Go,* 1990)

Values, Ethics, and Charity

Businesses get it: charity is good for business. According to the Council on Foundations, more than two thousand corporate foundations contribute in excess of $12 billion a year to nonprofit organizations in cash, goods, and services. Business philanthropy generates invaluable publicity, illuminating corporate fulfillment of community responsibility. Workers, too, have taken a hard look at their own values and ethics, and are trying to determine how they fit into the workplace. "Social responsibility" is the new buzzword, with both employees and the world at large benefitting, as the quotes below show.

Don't be foolish with the money you've made. No big cars. Second, remember who you are. Stay humble and be generous. It's the right thing to do, and it feels good.

—T. Boone Pickens, Texas oilman and investor

One of the deep secrets of life is that all that is really worth doing is what we do for others.

—Lewis Carroll, writer (from his book *Alice in Wonderland*, 1865)

We must intertwine business and ethics in a very fundamental way.

—Robert Bruner, business professor

In law a man is guilty when he violates the rights of others. In ethics he is guilty if he only thinks of doing so.

—Immanuel Kant, German philosopher

———◆———

Facebook was not originally created to be a company. It was built to accomplish a social mission—to make the world more open and connected.

—Mark Zuckerberg, cofounder and CEO of Facebook

———◆———

You must be the change you wish to see in the world.

—Mahatma Gandhi, Indian independence leader

It is a mistake for a man who wishes for happiness and to help others to think that he will wait until he has made a fortune before giving away money to deserving objects.

> —John D. Rockefeller, industrialist, cofounder of Standard Oil Co., and philanthropist

Relativity applies to physics, not ethics.

> —Albert Einstein, developer of the theory of relativity

All company bosses want a policy on corporate social responsibility. The positive effect is hard to quantify, but the negative consequences of a disaster are enormous.

> —Noreena Hertz, academic, economist, and author (from her article at newstatesman.com, June 21, 1999)

Integrity has no need of rules.

—Albert Camus, French philosopher

———◆◆◆———

I like to bring people together so we don't waste opportunities and resources and keep doing the wrong things when we know better. Corporate America makes great things and things that can hurt us. They have to be part of the solutions. There's nothing to say you don't make a profit by doing good.

—Teresa Heinz, businesswoman and philanthropist

———◆◆◆———

Forcing people to be generous isn't humanitarian, effective, compassionate or moral. Only acts that are truly voluntary for all concerned can be truly compassionate.

—Harry Browne, director of public policy, American Liberty Foundation

Only a life lived in the service to others is worth living.
— Albert Einstein, developer of the theory of evolution

——◆——

Life is not about receiving. It's about giving, knowing that someone might learn, understand or grow that little bit from the experience.
—Peter Ellis, author

——◆——

If we only have great companies, we will merely have a prosperous society, not a great one. Economic growth and power are the means, not the definition, of a great nation.
—Jim Collins, business consultant, author, and lecturer

We're starting with our own carbon footprint. Not nothing. But much of what we're doing is already, or soon will be, little more than the standard way of doing business. We can do something that's unique, different from just any other company. We can set an example, and we can reach our audiences. Our audience's carbon footprint is 10,000 times bigger than ours. That's the carbon footprint we want to conquer.

  —Rupert Murdoch, media mogul

<hr/>

It is time for corporate America to become "the third pillar" of social change in our society, complementing the first two pillars of government and philanthropy. We need the entire private sector to begin committing itself not just to making profits, but to fulfilling higher and larger purposes by contributing to building a better world.

  —Simon Mainwaring, advertising creative director and
  social media specialist (from mashable.com, April 22,
  2011)

For the triumph of good, we have to make a choice. We can enlist on the side of good by prospering, making money and using our wealth to help others.
—Rohinton Mistry, author

There are no second chances for those who violate the ethical code.
—Robert Slater, author

I used to use business to make money. But I've learned that business is a tool. You can use it to support what you believe in.
—Po Bronson, journalist and author

As more and more people wake up to the fact that further growth does not necessarily bring improvements in quality of life (and often exactly the opposite), sustainability is going to become one of the key characteristics with which places want to be associated.

—Jonathon Porritt, British environmentalist and writer

I believe it is a religious duty to get all the money you can, fairly and honestly; to keep all you can, and to give away all you can.

—John D. Rockefeller, industrialist, cofounder of Standard Oil Co., and philanthropist

Successful people have a social responsibility to make the world a better place and not just take from it.

—Carrie Underwood, singer-songwriter

He profits most who serves best.
—Arthur F. Sheldon, businessman

———————

Making money is marvelous, and I love doing it, and I do it reasonably well, but it doesn't have the gripping vitality that you have when you deal with the happiness of human life and with human deprivation.
—Edgar Bronfman Sr., CEO of Seagram's and philanthropist

———————

Making money is a happiness. And that's a great incentive. Making other people happy is a super-happiness.
—Muhammad Yunus, Nobel Peace Prize winner

I've always said that the better off you are, the more responsibility you have for helping others. Just as I think it's important to run companies well, with a close eye to the bottom line, I think you have to use your entrepreneurial experience to make corporate philanthropy effective.

—Carlos Slim Helu, billionaire Mexican industrialist

As you grow older, you will discover that you have two hands, one for helping yourself, the other for helping others.

—Audrey Hepburn, actress

I believe the power to make money is a gift of God . . . to be developed and used to the best of our ability for the good of mankind. Having been endowed with the gift I possess, I believe it is my duty to make money and still more money and to use the money I make for the good of my fellow man according to the dictates of my conscience.

—John D. Rockefeller, industrialist, cofounder of Standard Oil Co., and philanthropist

Men are rich only as they give. He who gives great service gets great rewards.

—Elbert Hubbard, writer, publisher, artist, and philosopher

You will get all you want in life if you help enough other people get what they want.

—Zig Ziglar, motivational speaker

Successful people are always looking for opportunities to help others. Unsuccessful people are always asking, "What's in it for me?"

—Brian Tracy, author

I want to know surely in giving that I am putting money where it will do most good.

—John D. Rockefeller, industrialist, cofounder of Standard Oil Co., and philanthropist

———◆———

Success isn't about how much money you make. It's about the difference you make in people's lives.

—Michelle Obama, First Lady

———◆———

No business which depends for existence on paying less than living wages to its workers has any right to continue in this country.

—Franklin D. Roosevelt, US president

Multinational corporations do control. They control the politicians. They control the media. They control the pattern of consumption, entertainment, thinking. They're destroying the planet and laying the foundation for violent outbursts and racial division.

—Jerry Brown, Governor of California

It's ridiculous to talk about freedom in a society dominated by huge corporations. What kind of freedom is there inside a corporation? They're totalitarian institutions—you take orders from above and maybe give them to people below you. There's about as much freedom as under Stalinism.

—Noam Chomsky, linguist, philosopher, cognitive scientist, historian, social critic, and political activist

The higher the buildings, the lower the morals.

—Noel Coward, playwright

If the firms that employ an increasing majority of the population are driven solely to satisfy the owner's greed at the expense of working conditions, of the stability of the community, and of the health of the environment, chances are that the quality of our lives will be worse than it is now.

—Mihaly Csikszentmihalyi, Hungarian psychologist

—————◆—————

Corporate America cannot afford to remain silent or passive about the downward spiral we are undergoing. It cannot turn a blind eye to how difficult the experience of life is for so many of their customers.

—Simon Mainwaring, advertising creative director and social media specialist (from website Mashable, April 22, 2011)

—————◆—————

Wall Street, the banks, and corporate America have been able to call the shots here. They control our members of Congress and they get what they want.

—Michael Moore, filmmaker

Morality is of the highest importance—but for us, not for God.

—Albert Einstein, developer of the theory of relativity

Capitalism is destroying the planet. The two old tricks that dug it out of past crises—War and Shopping—simply will not work.

—Arundhati Roy, author

And sometimes I actually start to think human life is just as cheap to corporate America as animal life, so long as there are big profits to be made.

—Tom Scholz, musician

When you stop to think about it, it is apparent that we do consider corporations to be ethical entities, at least in some measure.

—Wade Rowland, Canadian science, technology, and travel writer

Now you have a choice: we can give more tax breaks to corporations that ship jobs overseas, or we can start rewarding companies that open new plants and train new workers and create new jobs here, in the United States of America.

—Barack Obama, US president

Corporations are poisoning our air and water while at the same time lining the pockets of elected officials with political contributions.

—Gloria Reuben, actress

The idea that each corporation can be a feudal monarchy and yet behave in its corporate action like a democratic citizen concerned for the world we live in is one of the great absurdities of our time.

—Kim Stanley Robinson, science fiction writer

I do not believe maximizing profits for the investors is the only acceptable justification for all corporate actions. The investors are not the only people who matter. Corporations can exist for purposes other than simply maximizing profits.

—John Mackey, cofounder and CEO of Whole Foods Market

I think the people should have a right to boycott whoever they want to boycott without the government making them into criminals and try to protect corporations from people. They should protect people from corporations.

—Ziggy Marley, musician

Corporations are not legal "persons" with constitutional rights and freedoms of their own, but legal fictions that we created and must therefore control.

　　—Kalle Lasn, Estonian-Canadian filmmaker, author, and magazine editor

I hope we shall crush in its birth the aristocracy of our moneyed corporations which dare already to challenge our government to a trial by strength, and bid defiance to the laws of our country.

　　—Thomas Jefferson, US founding father and president

We give more economic aid to multinational corporations to increase their profits than we do to all the countries in the world combined.

　　—Michael Hogan, author

When a company is not being guided by the products they make and what the customers need, but by how they can manipulate the system—get regulations on their competitors, or mandates on using their products, or eliminating foreign competition—it just lowers the overall standard of living and hurts the disadvantaged the most.

—Charles Koch, co-owner of Koch Industries

A funny thing happened to the First Amendment on its way to the public forum. According to the Supreme Court, money is now speech and corporations are now people. But when real people without money assemble to express their dissatisfaction with the political consequences of this, they're treated as public nuisances and evicted.

—Robert Reich, secretary of labor, professor, and author

In business everything is subject to change—people, products, buildings, machinery, everything—except principles. To paraphrase Thomas Jefferson, in matters of principle, stand like a rock; in other matters, swim with the current. So, while I strongly advocate flexibility, when it comes to principles we must stand firm.

—Mary Kay Ash, founder of Mary Kay Cosmetics

It has become dramatically clear that the foundation of corporate integrity is personal integrity.

—Sam DiPiazza, CEO of PricewaterhouseCoopers

I think one of the most misunderstood things about business in America is that people are either doing things for altruistic reasons or they are greedy and selfish, just after profit. That type of dichotomy portrays a false image of business . . . the whole idea is to do both.

—John Mackey, cofounder and CEO of Whole Foods Market

Business is about profit, yes—and it is about more than profit: at its best, it is about expanding the possibilities of humanity.

—Jon Miller, author

All of our political parties are bought and paid for by corporate America, Wall Street, and the wealthy interests. The Republican Party more so, but the Democrats take their share of the loot, too.

—Michael Moore, filmmaker

It was here I learnt that corporate principles and military principles are basically the same. Insulation. Illusion. Hype. Activity.

—Tarun J. Tejpal, Indian journalist, publisher, novelist and editor

I believe that if corporate America expects consumer confidence to be restored, they must first be honest with us.

—Bennie Thompson, US congressman

⟝⬩⟞

Nothing is illegal if one hundred businessmen decide to do it.

—Andrew Young, US ambassador to the UN and Atlanta mayor

⟝⬩⟞

Next to doing the right thing, the most important thing is to let people know you are doing the right thing.

—John D. Rockefeller, industrialist, cofounder of Standard Oil Co., and philanthropist

The businessman is only tolerable so long as his gains can be held to bear some relation to what, roughly and in some sense, his activities have contributed to society.

—John Maynard Keynes, economist

Since most corporate competitors have the same problems with sustainability and social reputation, it's worth trying to solve them together.

—Simon Mainwaring, advertising creative director and social media specialist (from his book *We First: How Brands and Consumers Use Social Media to Build a Better World,* 2011)

For a successful entrepreneur it can mean extreme wealth. But with extreme wealth comes extreme responsibility. And the responsibility for me is to invest in creating new businesses, create jobs, employ people, and to put money aside to tackle issues where we can make a difference.

—Sir Richard Branson, billionaire entrepreneur and founder of Virgin Airlines

If you abandon the political arena, somebody is going to be there. Corporations aren't going to go home and join the PTA. They are going to run things.

—Noam Chomsky, linguist, philosopher, cognitive scientist, historian, social critic, and political activist

———————

Real integrity is doing the right thing, knowing that nobody's going to know whether you did it or not.

—Oprah Winfrey, television mogul, television host, actress

———————

I'm not a do-gooder. It embarrassed me to be classified as a humanitarian. I simply take part in activities that I believe in.

—Gregory Peck, actor

Ethics is knowing the difference between what you have a right to do and what is right to do.

—Potter Stewart, justice of the US Supreme Court

We are a company that lives and breathes a philosophy that's centered on not only making sound business decisions but also personally and professionally finding ways to contribute to the well-being of society. We are also a company that understands community.

—Magic Johnson, NBA legend

Many persons have an idea that one cannot be in business and lead an upright life, whereas the truth is that no one succeeds in business to any great extent, who misleads or misrepresents.

—John Wanamaker, department-store magnate

Fame is vapor, popularity an accident, riches take wings. Only one thing endures, and that is character.
—Horace Greeley, editor

———❖———

Corporations should not be charged with the responsibility of administering aspects of human life that properly have nothing to do with profit.
—Wade Rowland, Canadian science, technology, and travel writer

———❖———

Humanitarianism consists in never sacrificing a human being to a purpose.
—Albert Schweitzer, theologian and philosopher

If you build that foundation, both the moral and the ethical foundation, as well as the business foundation, and the experience foundation, then the building won't crumble.

> —Henry Kravis, cofounder of Kohlberg Kravis Roberts & Co.

Business social responsibility should not be coerced; it is a voluntary decision that the entrepreneurial leadership of every company must make on its own.

> —John Mackey, cofounder and CEO of Whole Foods Market

Try not to become a man of success. Rather become a man of value.

> —Albert Einstein, developer of the theory of relativity

Engaging in social business is beneficial to a company because it leverages on business competencies to address social issues, involves one-time investment with sustainable results, and produces other positive effects such as employee motivation and improved organizational culture.

—Muhammad Yunus, Nobel Peace Prize winner

Goodwill is the only asset that competition cannot undersell or destroy.

—Marshall Field, founder of Marshall Field department stores

The man who has won millions at the cost of his conscience is a failure.

—B. C. Forbes, founder of *Forbes* magazine

Do we need weapons to fight wars? Or do we need wars to create markets for weapons?

—Arundhati Roy, author

———◆———

I believe that every right implies a responsibility; every opportunity an obligation; every possession a duty.

—John D. Rockefeller, industrialist, cofounder of Standard Oil Co., and philanthropist

———◆———

It is difficult, but not impossible, to conduct strictly honest business.

—Mahatma Gandhi, Indian independence leader

Transforming a brand into a socially responsible leader doesn't happen overnight by simply writing new marketing and advertising strategies. It takes effort to identify a vision that your customers will find credible and aligned with their values.

—Simon Mainwaring, advertising creative director and social media specialist (from website Mashable, April 22, 2011)

———

We can't help everyone, but everyone can help someone.

—Ronald Reagan, US president

List of Speakers Quoted

A

—Ziad K. Abdelnour, investment banker and financier

—Paula Abdul, singer-songwriter

—Jay Abraham, author and business executive

—Charles Adams, advertising executive

—Phillip Adams, film producer, broadcaster, and writer

—Tom Ajamie and Bruce Kelly, coauthors

—Louis Agassiz, author, doctor, scientist, and academic

—Howard Aiken, physicist and computer pioneer

—Roger Ailes, chairman of Fox News Channel

—Lailah Gifty Akita, founder of Smart Youth Volunteers Foundation

—Andy Albright, author

—Louisa May Alcott, novelist and poet

—Alan Alda, actor, director, and writer

—Scott Alexander, author

—Muhammad Ali, boxer and humanitarian

—David Allen, author

—Marc Allen, author and publisher

—Robert G. Allen, author

—Woody Allen, actor and filmmaker

—Doug Anderson, author

—Mario Andretti, racing driver

—Maya Angelou, poet, author, and civil rights activist

—Kofi Annan, Secretary-General of the United Nations

—Walter Annenberg, publisher, philanthropist, and diplomat

—Adam Ant, singer and musician

—Robert Anthony, author and psychologist

—Paul Arden, advertising executive

—Aristophanes, Greek playwright

—Giorgio Armani, fashion designer

—Dee Dee Artner, author and behavioral expert

—Mary Kay Ash, founder of Mary Kay Cosmetics

—Laura Ashley, fashion designer

—Isaac Asimov, author and professor of biochemistry

—Ehab Atalla, author, entrepreneur, and investor

—Dane Atkinson, CEO of SumAll

—Red Auerbach, legendary coach of the Boston Celtics

—Jane Austen, English novelist

—Israelmore Ayivor, writer

B

—Leo Babauta, author

—Isaac Babel, Russian language journalist, playwright, and short story writer

—David Bach, financial consultant

—Francis Bacon, English philosopher, statesman, scientist, jurist, orator, and author

—David Bailey, artist

—Lester Bangs, music journalist, critic, author, and musician

—Katherine Barchetti, founder of K. Barchetti Shops (Pittsburgh)

—Dave Barry, author and columnist

—Maria Bartiromo, business television anchor

—Bernard Baruch, financier, stock investor, philanthropist, and statesman

—Frederic Bastiat, French liberal theorist, legislator, and economist

—Warren Beatty, actor

—Jonathan Becher, chief digital officer of SAP

—Samuel Beckett, novelist, playwright, theatre director and poet

—Henry Ward Beecher, Congregationalist clergyman and social reformer

—Alexander Graham Bell, chief inventor of the telephone

—Chip Bell, founder of Chip Bell Group

—Scott Belsky, entrepreneur and author

—Robert Benchley, author

—William J. Bennett, U.S. Secretary of Education

—Milton Berle, comedian and actor

—Irving Berlin, composer

—William Bernbach, advertising legend and cofounder of the Doyle Dane Bernbach agency

—Al Bernstein, journalist and sportscaster

—Leonard Bernstein, composer/conductor

—Jeff Bezos, founder of Amazon.com

—Ambrose Bierce, journalist and author

—Stanley Bing, pen name of Gil Schwartz, business humorist and novelist

—Clarence Birdseye, inventor, entrepreneur, and pioneer of the frozen foods industry

—Ken Blanchard, author and management expert

—Jim Blasingame, author

—Peter Block, author and business consultant

—Toby Bloomberg, strategy and social media consultant

—Laszlo Bock, Google executive

—Humphrey Bogart, actor

—Louis Boone, author

—Julia Boorstin, senior media and entertainment correspondent, CNBC

—Nelson Boswell, self-help author

— Christian Nestell Bovee, writer

—Chris Bradford, author, professional musician, and black belt martial artist

—Bill Bradley, NBA star and U.S. senator

—Bernard Branson, author

—Richard Branson, billionaire entrepreneur and founder of Virgin Airlines

—David Brinkley, news anchor for NBC and ABC

—Claude M. Bristol, author

—Steuart Henderson Britt, marketing consultant, psychologist, and author

—Chris Brogan and Julien Smith, coauthors

—Edgar Bronfman Sr., CEO of Seagram's and philanthropist

—Po Bronson, journalist and author

—Joyce Brothers, psychologist and advice columnist

—Derby Brown

—H. Jackson Brown Jr., author

—Jerry Brown, Governor of California

—Les Brown, songwriter, orchestra leader, and author

—Pat Brown, Governor of California

—Harry Browne, director of public policy, American Liberty Foundation

—Robert Bruner, business professor

—Diane Bryant, Intel Corp. executive

—Paul "Bear" Bryant, legendary Alabama football coach

—Mark Buckingham and Curt Coffman, coauthors

—Gene Buckley, president of Sikorsky Aircraft

—Warren Buffett, legendary investor and CEO of Berkshire Hathaway

—Lois McMaster Bujold, author

—Thomas J. Burrell, founder of Burrell Communications

—Warren E. Burger, Chief Justice of the US Supreme Court

—James E. Burke, CEO of Johnson & Johnson

—Leo Burnett, founder of Leo Burnett Worldwide ad agency

—Ursula Burns, CEO of Xerox

—Aaron Burr, US Vice President

—Nolan Bushnell, engineer and founder of Atari Inc. and Chuck E. Cheese's Pizza-Time Theaters

—Samuel Butler, novelist

C

—Herman Cain, Republican presidential aspirant

—Mona Caird, Scottish novelist, essayist, and feminist

—David Campbell, author

—Albert Camus, French philosopher

—Jack Canfield, author and entrepreneur

—Truman Capote, novelist, screenwriter, playwright, and actor

—Grant Cardone, motivational speaker and author

—Thomas Carlyle, Scottish philosopher, essayist, satirist, and historian.

—Jan Carlzon, CEO of SAS

—Andrew Carnegie, steel industrialist

—Dale Carnegie, writer and lecturer

—Evangeline Caridas, consultant

—Alexis Carrel, French surgeon and biologist

—Lewis Carroll, writer

—Jim Carrey, actor and comedian

—Margaret Carty, Oregon politician

—Johnny Cash, country singer

—Warren Cassell Jr., Caribbean entrepreneur

—Carlos Castaneda, author

—Richard Cecil, Evangelical Anglican priest

—Gurbaksh Chahal, entrepreneur and author

—Chanakya, Indian teacher, philosopher, royal advisor, economist, and jurist

—Raymond Chandler, novelist and screenwriter

—Coco Chanel, fashion designer

—Ha-Joon Chang, South Korean economist

—Kenneth Chang, *New York Times* journalist

—Roy D. Chapin Jr., chairman and CEO of American Motors Corporation

—Brian Chesky, cofounder and CEO of Airbnb

—Lord Chesterfield, British statesman, diplomat, and wit

—Lydia M. Child, abolitionist, women's rights activist, novelist, and journalist

—Noam Chomsky, linguist, philosopher, cognitive scientist, historian, social critic, and political activist

—Rehan Choudhry, founder of Life Is Beautiful, Las Vegas music festival

—Winston Churchill, former prime minister of the United Kingdom

—Bill Clinton, US President

—Hillary Clinton, US Secretary of State, US Senator, First Lady, and Presidential candidate

—Paulo Coelho, Brazilian lyricist and novelist

—Robert Collier, self-help author

—Jim Collins, business consultant, author, and lecturer

—Confucius, Chinese philosopher

—Charles Caleb Colton, English cleric, writer, and collector

—Scott Cook, founder of Intuit Inc.

—Paul Cookson, poet-performer

—Calvin Coolidge, US President

—Alice Cooper, rock musician

—John-Francois Cope, French politician

—Barbara Corcoran, businesswoman, investor, syndicated columnist, author, and television personality

—Pierre Corneille, French dramatist

—E. Joseph Cossman, marketing impresario and author

—Katie Couric, television and Yahoo! news anchor

—Stephen Covey, educator, author, and businessman

—Noel Coward, playwright

—Simon Cowell, television producer

—Robert Crandall, airline executive

—Dennis Crowley, CEO of Foursquare

—Mark Cuban, owner of Dallas Mavericks, Landmark Theatres, and Magnolia Pictures

—George Cukor, film director

—Mihaly Csikszentmihalyi, Hungarian psychologist

D

—Nick D'Aloisio, English computer programmer and Internet entrepreneur

—Andrew Darrah, author

—Charles Darwin, developer of the theory of evolution

—William H. Davidow, high-technology industry executive and venture capitalist

—Bette Davis, actress

—Clive Davis, music executive

—Leonardo Da Vinci, artist

—Christine Day, CEO of Luvo

—Ellen DeGeneres, talk show host and actress

—Noel DeJesus, author

—John Paul DeJoria, businessman

—Michael Dell, founder of Dell Computers

—Jayson Demers, entrepreneur and columnist

—W. Edwards Deming, engineer, scholar, author, and management consultant

—Democritus, ancient Greek philosopher

—Felix Dennis, publisher and poet

—Junot Diaz, writer and creative writing professor

—Sam DiPiazza, CEO of PricewaterhouseCoopers

—Walt Disney, founder of Walt Disney Studios and theme parks

—Benjamin Disraeli, British Prime Minister and writer

—Lloyd Dobens and Clare Crawford-Mason, coauthors

—Amanda Donohoe, actress

—Richard Dooling, novelist and screenwriter

—Tony Dorsett, NFL football player

—Norman Douglas, British writer

—Frederick Douglass, African-American abolitionist, orator, and writer

—Peter F. Drucker, management consultant, educator, and author

—Alexandre Dumas, writer

—William Durant, cofounder of General Motors

—Dr. Wayne W. Dyer, philosopher, self-help author, and motivational speaker

E

—Thomas Edison, inventor

—Sir John Egan, British industrialist

—Albert Einstein, developer of the theory of relativity

—Ansel Elgort, actor and DJ

—Charles W. Eliot, Harvard University president

—Walter Elliott, priest and author

—Havelock Ellis, English physician, writer, intellectual, and social reformer

—Peter Ellis, author

—Larry Ellison, cofounder of Oracle Corporation

—Ralph Ellison, novelist

—Melinda Emerson, founder and CEO of Quintessence Multimedia

—Ralph Waldo Emerson, philosopher, poet, and essayist

—Eminem, rapper

—Emenike Emmanuel, Nigerian soccer player

—Brian Eno, musician, composer, and producer

—Sven-Göran Eriksson Swedish football manager and former player

—Jonas Eriksson, writer

—Robert Estabrook, journalist

—Doug Evelyn, Smithsonian Institution executive

—Sam Ewing, professional baseball player

—Dr. O. Ezekiel, minister

F

—Tim Fargo, CEO of Tweet Jukebox

—Nauman Faridi, Internet technologist

—William Feather, publisher and author

—Diane Feinstein, US Senator

—Owen Felltham, English writer

—Jerry Della Femina, advertising executive and restaurateur

—Tony Fernandes, entrepreneur

—Abel Ferrara, filmmaker

—Tina Fey, actress and comedian

—Richard P. Feynman, physicist and winner of the Nobel Prize in Physics

—Marshall Field, founder of Marshall Fields department store

—Debbi Fields, founder of Mrs. Fields Bakeries

—Harvey S. Firestone, founder of the Firestone Tire and Rubber Company

—John Fisher, British admiral

—Janet Fitch, author

—F. Scott Fitzgerald, novelist

—Zelda Fitzgerald, socialite and novelist

—Mary Parker Follett, business thinker and author

—Malcolm S. Forbes, publisher of *Forbes* magazine

—Henry Ford, founder of Ford Motor Company

—Tom Ford, fashion designer

—William A. Foster, World War II–era Medal of Honor awardee

—Marci G. Fox, psychologist

—Erwin Fran, author

—Anatole France, poet and journalist

—Benjamin Franklin, US founding father and inventor

—Milton Friedman, economist

—Jerry Fritz, director of Management Institute University of Wisconsin

—D. Allan Fromme, psychologist, teacher, and writer

—Robert Frost, poet

—Northrop Frye, Canadian literary

—R. Buckminster Fuller, architect, systems theorist, author, designer, and inventor

—Thomas Fuller, English physician, writer, and adage collector

G

—Noel Gallagher, English musician

—Vincent A. Gallagher, author and safety expert

—Kim Garst, founder and CEO of Boom! Social

—Bill Gates, cofounder of Microsoft and philanthropist

—David Geffen, entertainment mogul

—Harold S. Geneen, chairman of ITT Corporation

—Balthazar Getty, actor

—J. Paul Getty, founder of Getty Oil

—Peter Gibbons, character in the movie Office Space

—Althea Gibson, pioneer black tennis player

—King Gillette, founder of the Gillette Safety Razor Company

—Jeffrey Gitomer, author

—William B. Given Jr., author

—Barbara Glacel, executive coach

—Seth Godin, author, entrepreneur, and public speaker

—Johann Wolfgang von Goethe, German writer and statesman

—James Goldsmith, Anglo-French billionaire financier

—Samuel Gompers, labor union leader

—Leon Gorman, chairman of L.L. Bean

—Baltasar Gracián, Spanish Jesuit author

—David Graeber, author, anthropologist and anarchist activist

—Francis Gray, Massachusetts politician

—Horace Greeley, editor

—John Green, author

—Philip Green, British businessman and the chairman of Arcadia Group

—Jerry Gregoire, chief information officer, Dell Computer

—Wayne Gretzky, hockey great

—Skylar Grey, singer and songwriter

—Merv Griffin, talk show host, entertainer, and media mogul

—Andrew Grove, chairman and CEO of Intel

H

—Doris Haddock, political activist

—Nirrimi Joy Hakanson, fashion photographer

—J.B.S. Haldane, scientist

—Robert Half, founder of Robert Half International

—Gary Hamel, management expert

—Laurell K. Hamilton, fantasy and romance writer

—Mia Hamm, professional soccer player

—Isaiah Hankel, author and speaker

—David Heinemeier Hansson, Danish computer programmer

—Amber Harding, multimedia sports journalist

—Chris Hardwick, television host, stand-up comedian, actor, and writer

—Jerry Harvey, cofounder of Australia retailing chain Harvey Norman Holdings

—Sir John Harvey-Jones, English businessman

—Stanley Hauerwas, theologian, ethicist, and public intellectual

—Paul Hawken, environmentalist, entrepreneur, author, and activist

—S.I. Hayakawa, US Senator

—Denis Healey, motivational speaker, writer, and consultant

—Georg Wilhelm Friedrich Hegel, philosopher

—Jascha Heifetz, virtuoso violinist

—Teresa Heinz, businesswoman and philanthropist

—Carlos Slim Helu, billionaire Mexican industrialist

—Ernest Hemingway, novelist

—Bruce Henderson, founder of the Boston Consulting Group

—Katharine Hepburn, actress

—Noreena Hertz, academic, economist, and author

—John Heywood, English playwright

—Kris A. Hiatt, author

—Napoleon Hill, pioneer of the modern genre of personal success

—Edmund Hillary, New Zealand mountaineer, explorer, and philanthropist

—Conrad Hilton, founder of Hilton Hotels

—Eric Hoffer, philosopher

—Michael Hogan, author

—Homer, Greek poet

—Ron Holland, author

—Oliver Wendell Holmes, US Supreme Court justice

—John W. Holt, author

—Lou Holtz, college football coaching legend

—Russel Honore, US military officer

—Herbert Hoover, US President

—Drew Houston, founder and CEO of Dropbox

—Elbert Hubbard, writer, publisher, artist, and philosopher

—Arianna Huffington, founder of the *Huffington Post*

—Hubert H. Humphrey, US Vice President

—Thomas Huxley, English biologist

I

—Lee Iacocca, chairman and CEO of Chrysler Motors

—Carl Icahn, investor

—Bob Iger, chairman and CEO, Walt Disney Co.

—Jeffrey Immelt, chairman and CEO of GE

—Shafqat Islam, CEO of NewsCred

—Ken Iverson, author

—Steven Ivy, attorney and entrepreneur

J

—Andrew Jackson, US President

—Phil Jackson, NBA coach and team executive

—Bianca Jagger, social and human rights advocate

—William James, philosopher and psychologist

—Francine Jay, author and minimalist

—Jay-Z, rapper and entertainment mogul

—Thomas Jefferson, Founding Father and President

—Steve Jobs, cofounder of Apple and Pixar Animation

—Jimmy Johnson, professional football coach

—Magic Johnson, NBA legend

—Michael Bassey Johnson, author

—Samuel Johnson, British author

—Sheila Johnson, cofounder of Black Entertainment Television

—Stewart B. Johnson, artist

—E. Stanley Jones, author and Methodist Christian missionary and theologian

—Mike Jones, CEO of Science Inc.

—David Starr Jordan, ichthyologist, educator, eugenicist, and peace activist

—Michael Jordan, NBA legend

—Joseph Joubert, French moralist and essayist

—H. Stanley Judd, author

—Carl Gustav Jung, Swiss psychologist and lead author of *Memories, Dreams, Reflections*

—Jerry Junkins, CEO of Texas Instruments

K

—Franz Kafka, novelist and short story writer

—Amit Kalantri, author

—Oran Kangas, author

—Immanuel Kant, German philosopher

—Chester L. Karrass, negotiations expert

—Debra Kaye, composer

—Helen Keller, journalist, author, and activist for the blind

—Kevin Kelly, author

—Leo-Arthur Kelmenson, ad executive

—John F. Kennedy, US President

—Joseph P. Kennedy, businessman, diplomat, and patriarch of the Kennedy political clan

—Robert F. Kennedy, US Senator and US Attorney General

—Rose F. Kennedy, Kennedy family matriarch

—Corita Kent, Catholic nun, artist, and educator

—Dave Kerpen, entrepreneur, author, and reality television personality

—John Maynard Keynes, economist

—Vinod Khosla, cofounder of Sun Microsystems

—Nikita Khrushchev, Soviet leader

—Kijung Kim, South Korean badminton player

—Billie Jean King, world champion tennis player

—Martin Luther King Jr., civil rights leader

—Stephen King, author

—Dennis Kinlaw, theological educator

—Sophie Kinsella, author

—W.P. Kinsella, novelist and short story writer

—Jarod Kintz, author

—Robert Kiyosaki, entrepreneur and author

—George Kneller, philosophy professor

—Phil Knight, Nike founder

—Charles Koch, co-owner of Koch Industries

—Richard Koch, British author, speaker, and investor

—Alfie Kohn, author and lecturer

—Rem Koolhaas, Dutch architect, architectural theorist, urbanist, and Harvard professor

—Jack Kornfield, author and teacher

—Jan Koum, Internet entrepreneur and computer programmer

—Jeramey Kraatz, author

—Henry Kravis, investor and financier

—Ray Kroc, chairman of McDonald's

—Louis Kronenberger, critic and author

—Mike Krzyzewski, college basketball coach

—Nirmalya Kumar, professor of marketing and director of Aditya Birla India Centre, London Business School

—Milan Kundera, novelist

—Joseph C. Kunz Jr., entrepreneur and author

L

—John Lahr, senior drama critic at *The New Yorker* magazine

—Dr. Edwin Land, cofounder of the Polaroid Corporation

—Jaron Lanier, computer scientist, author, and composer

—Kalle Lasn, Estonian-Canadian filmmaker, author, and magazine editor

—Ralph Lauren, fashion designer

—Estee Lauder, cofounder of Estée Lauder Companies

—Irving Paul Lazar, talent agent

—Stephen Butler Leacock, Canadian teacher, political scientist, writer, and humorist

—Michael LeBoeuf, business professor and author

—Bruce Lee, actor

—Patrick Lencioni, author and management expert

—Stew Leonard, retailer

—Theodore Levitt, economist, professor at Harvard Business School, and author

—Joshua E. Leyenhorst, owner of Promadim Promotional Products, British Columbia

—Rensis Likert, social psychologist

—Doris Lilly, gossip columnist

—Ryan Lilly, writer

—Abraham Lincoln, US President

—Dr. Henry Link, employment psychologist

—Betty Liu, Bloomberg TV anchor

—John Locke, English philosopher and physician

—George Lois, advertising legend

—Vince Lombardi, professional football coaching legend

—Jonathan Long, founder and CEO of Market Domination Media

— Wadsworth Longfellow, poet

—Audre Lorde, writer, feminist, and civil rights activist

—George Claude Lorimer, pastor

—Jason Love, marketing executive

—George Lucas, creator of *Star Wars* and *Indiana Jones*

—Henry R. Luce, founder of *Time* magazine

—Peter Lynch, Fidelity Fund manager

—Nick Lyons, teacher, writer, publisher, and dad

—Edward George Bulwer Lytton, novelist

M

—John McAfee, software entrepreneur

—Gen. Douglas MacArthur, U.S. military leader

—Thomas Babington Macaulay, a British historian and Whig politician

—Terry McAuliffe, governor of Virginia

—Matthew McConaughey, actor

—Colin McEnroe, columnist and radio host

—Bryant McGill, author

—Machiavelli, Italian Renaissance political philosopher

—Harvey Mackay, author and founder of Mackay Mitchell Envelope Co.

—Ian MacKaye, singer, songwriter, and guitarist

—Max McKeown, English writer and consultant

—John Mackey, cofounder and CEO of Whole Foods Market

—Mignon McLaughlin, journalist and author

—Marshall McLuhan, Canadian philosopher, futurist, and communications theorist

—Peter McWilliams, self-help author and marijuana legalization advocate

—Sydney Madwed, public speaker, poet, lyricist, and author

—Bill Maher, comedian and television host

—Simon Mainwaring, advertising creative director and social media specialist

—Og Mandino, author

—Henning Mankell, Swedish crime writer

—Marya Mannes, author and critic

—Steve Maraboli, author and behavioral scientist

—Orison Swett Marden, inspirational author and founder of *SUCCESS* magazine

—Orison Swett Marden, inspirational author and founder

—Ziggy Marley, musician

—Scott Marquart, author

—Julianna Margulies, actress

—Jacques Maritain, French Catholic philosopher

—Art Markman, professor of psychology and marketing

—Paul Marsden, writer and businessman

—Peter Marshall, author

—Ajaero Tony Martins, Nigerian entrepreneur and investor

—Karl Marx, philosopher, economist, and revolutionary socialist

—Andrew Mason, founder and CEO of Groupon Inc.

—Andre Maurois, French author

—John C. Maxwell, author, speaker, and pastor

—Marissa Mayer, CEO of Yahoo!

—Joyce Maynard, novelist and journalist

—Margaret Mead, anthropologist

—Andrew Mellon, banker, industrialist, philanthropist, and US ambassador

—Herman Melville, novelist and poet

—Danny Meyer, restaurant entrepreneur

—Paul J. Meyer, founder of Success Motivation Institute

—Mary Mihalic, author

—Michael Milken, former financier

—Jon Miller, author

—Dan Millman, author and personal development lecturer

—C. Wright Mills, sociologist

—Lisa A. Mininni, author

—Kathryn Minshew, CEO and cofounder of The Muse

—Rohinton Mistry, author

—Lakshmi Mittal, Indian steel magnate

—Bob Moawad, author

—Mohammed, Prophet of Islam

—Mokokoma Mokhonoana, philosopher, social critic, graphic designer, and writer

—Luca Cordero di Montezemolo, former chairman of Fiat

—Michael Moore, filmmaker

—George L. Morrisey, author

—Nathan W. Morris, author and personal finance expert

—Daniel Patrick Moynihan, politician and sociologist

—Vishwas Mudagal, entrepreneur and author

—Malcolm Muggeridge, journalist and broadcaster

—Haruki Murakami, Japanese writer

—James Murdoch, CEO of 21st Century Fox

—Rupert Murdoch, media mogul

—Bill Murray, comedian and actor

—Chris Murray, author, inspirational speaker, and business coach

—Jim Murren, Chairman and CEO of MGM Resorts International

—Stan Musial, storied Hall of Fame player with the St. Louis Cardinals

—Elon Musk, founder of Tesla Motors and SpaceX

—Blake Mycoskie, founder of TOMS Shoes, author, and philanthropist

—Lorii Myers, author

—Nathan Myhrvold, Silicon Valley entrepreneur and investor

N

—Ogden Nash, poet

—George Nelson, industrial designer and a founder of American Modernism

—Willie Nelson, musician

—Friedrich Nietzsche, German philosopher, cultural critic, and poet

—Earl Nightingale, radio personality, writer, and author

—Richie Norton, author

—Robert Noyce, cofounder of Fairchild Semiconductor and Intel Corporation

O

—Barack Obama, US President

—Michelle Obama, First Lady

—Adolph S. Ochs, newspaper publisher

—Roger Von Oech, speaker, author, and toy-maker

—David Ogilvy, founder of Ogilvy & Mather ad agency

—Rasheed Ogunlaru, life coach, speaker, and author

—Georgia O'Keeffe, artist

—Martin Oliver, executive with Kwik-Fit Financial Service

—Laurence Olivier, actor

—Aristotle Onassis, Greek shipping magnate

—Ifeanyi Enoch Onuoha, author, inspirational speaker, and life coach

—Robert Orben, comedy writer

—Bill O'Reilly, television host, author, journalist, and a political commentator

—Paul Orfalea, founder of Kinko's

—Suze Orman, personal finance expert

—George Orwell, novelist, essayist, journalist, and critic

—Marc Ostrofsky, Internet entrepreneur and author

P

—David Packard, cofounder of Hewlett-Packard

—Larry Page, cofounder of Google

—Michael Palin, English comedian, actor, and writer

—James Parker, contributing editor, *Atlantic* magazine

—Sean Parker, cofounder of Facebook

—Cyril Northcote Parkinson, British naval historian and author

—Vikrant Parsai, author

—Dolly Parton, country singer

—James Parton, author

—Louis Pasteur, chemist and investor of pasteurization

—Peter J. Patsula, founder of Patsula Media and author

—John H. Patterson, National Cash Register Company

—Nkem Paul, author

—Linus Pauling, winner of the Nobel Prize in Chemistry and Nobel Peace Prize

—Terry Paulson, motivational speaker

—Norman Vincent Peale, minister, author, and a pioneer of "positive thinking"

—Gregory Peck, actor

—Noel Peebles, businessman and author

—J.C. Penney, founder of retail chain JCPenney

—Ross Perot, businessman and Reform Party presidential candidate

—Laurence J. Peter, author

—Tom Peters, author and business management expert

—Wilferd Peterson, author

—Michael Phelps, Olympic gold medalist

—William Lyon Phelps, author, critic, and scholar

—Mekhi Phifer, actor

—Pablo Picasso, artist

—T. Boone Pickens, Texas oilman and investor

—Mary Pickford, actress, writer, director, and producer

—Rick Pitino, college basketball coach

—Titus Maccius Plautus, Roman playwright

—Alexander Pope, English poet

—Jonathon Porritt, British environmentalist and writer

—Donald Porter, British Airways executive

—Colin Powell, US Secretary of State and Chairman of the Joint Chiefs of Staff

—Steven Pressfield, author

—J.B. Priestley, English playwright, novelist, biographer, literary critic, screenwriter, and broadcaster

Q

—Bill Quiseng, writer, speaker, hotel executive, and blogger

R

—A.R. Rahman, musician

—Tariq Ramadan, Swiss academic, philosopher, and writer

—Ron Rash, poet, short story writer, and novelist

—Tom Rath, author

—Mitch Ratliffe, writer

—Ronald Reagan, US President

—Bernice Johnson Reagon, singer

—Douglas B. Reeves, education author

—Robert Reich, Secretary of Labor, professor, and author

—Peter Relan, entrepreneur

—Gloria Reuben, actress

—Jef I. Richards, professor of advertising

—Pat Riley, professional basketball coach and executive

—Eloise Ristad, author

—César Ritz, founder of the Hôtel Ritz (Paris) and The Ritz Hotel (London)

—Rene Rivkin, Australian entrepreneur, investor, and investment adviser

—Harold Robbins, novelist

—Tony Robbins, motivational speaker, personal finance instructor, and self-help author.

—Lord Robens, chairman of the National Coal Board, United Kingdom

—Alan G. Robinson, business executive

—Ken Robinson, English author and international advisor on art education

—Kim Stanley Robinson, science fiction writer

—David Rockefeller, banker

—John D. Rockefeller, industrialist, cofounder of Standard Oil Co., and philanthropist

—Anita Roddick, founder of The Body Shop

—Will Rogers, American cowboy, vaudeville performer, humorist, newspaper columnist, social commentator, and stage and motion picture actor

—Jim Rohn, entrepreneur, author and motivational speaker

—Henry Rollins, musician, actor, television and radio host, and comedian

—Mickey Rooney, actor and comedian

—Eleanor Roosevelt, US First Lady

—Franklin D. Roosevelt, US President

—Theodore Roosevelt, US President

—George Ross, Trump Organization executive

—Wade Rowland, Canadian science, technology, and travel writer

—Arundhati Roy, author

—Gretchen Rubin, author, blogger, and speaker

—Michael Rubin, e-commerce entrepreneur

—John Russell, president of Harley Davidson, Europe

—Babe Ruth, baseball legend

—Paul Ryan, Speaker of the US House of Representatives

S

—Carl Sagan, astronomer, cosmologist, astrophysicist, and author

—N.V. Sakhardande, author and management expert

—Mark Sanborn, author and entrepreneur

—Sheryl Sandberg, chief operating officer of Facebook

—Betsy Sanders, Nordstrom executive and author

—Colonel Sanders, founder of Kentucky Fried Chicken

—George Santayana, philosopher, essayist, poet, and novelist

—Rodrigo Santoro, Brazilian actor

—Vidal Sassoon, hair care mogul

—Ryunosuke Satoro, Japanese writer

—Elizabeth Grace Saunders, time-management coach

—Eric Schiffer, author and entrepreneur

—Eric Schmidt, executive chairman of Alphabet Inc., formerly Google

—Tom Scholz, musician

—Howard Schultz, CEO of Starbucks

—Horst Schulze, president of the Ritz Carlton Hotels

—Charles M. Schwab, steel magnate

—Charles R. Schwab, founder of Charles Schwab Corp.

—Robert L. Schwartz, author and Harvard professor emeritus

—Arnold Schwarzenegger, actor and Governor of California

—Albert Schweitzer, theologian and philosopher

—Seneca, Roman Stoic philosopher, statesman, and dramatist

—Dr. Seuss, children's author

—Tahir Shah, Anglo-Afghan Indian author and journalist

—Robert S. Sharma, Canadian self-help writer

—Gena Showalter, romance writer

—Jacques Seguela, cofounder of French advertising agency RSCG

—Jerry Seinfeld, comedian, actor, writer, and producer

—Maurice Setter, English soccer player

—Justin Sewell, author

—Tupac Shakur, rap music star

—George Bernard Shaw, Irish playwright, critic, and polemicist

—Arthur F. Sheldon, businessman

—Sidney Sheldon, author

— Edgar A. Shoaff, entrepreneur and motivational speaker

—Igor Sikorsky, Russian-American aviation pioneer

—Ben Silbermann, founder of Pinterest

—Gene Simmons, musician

—Herbert Simon, political scientist and economist

—Peter Sinclair, author

—Shiv Singh, senior brand executive, Visa Inc.

—Shandel Slaten, executive coach

—Robert Slater, author

—Samuel Smiles, Scottish author and political reformer

—Adam Smith, TV business commentator

—Benjamin R. Smith, author

—Doug Smith, author and team-building expert

—Jada Pinkett Smith, actress

—Sydney Smith, English essayist

—Wilbur Smith, novelist

—Steven Spielberg, filmmaker

—Mike Stackpole, science fiction author

—Roger Staubach, professional quarterback

—Casey Stengel, baseball legend

—Mattie Stepanek, poet

—David Stern, commissioner of the National Basketball Association

—Vilhjalmur Stefansson, Canadian explorer and ethnologist

—John Steinbeck, author

—Robert Louis Stevenson, Scottish poet and novelist

—Jimmy Stewart, actor

—Potter Stewart, Justice of the US Supreme Court

—Kevin Stirtz, author and web marketing consultant

—John Stoker, author

—Kerry Stokes, Australian broadcast billionaire

—Biz Stone, cofounder of Twitter

—W. Clement Stone, businessman, philanthropist, and self-help author

—Steve Stoute, advertising executive and marketing expert

—Billy Sunday, baseball professional turned evangelist

—James Surowiecki, journalist

—Marilyn Suttle, author and motivational speaker

—Jonathan Swift, Anglo-Irish satirist, essayist, political pamphleteer, poet, and cleric

—Charles R. Swindoll, evangelical Christian pastor, author, educator, and radio preacher

—Sandra Swinney, author

T

—Matt Taibbi, journalist

—Savielly Tartakower, Polish and French chess grandmaster

—Rick Tate, author and customer-loyalty strategist

—Tarun J. Tejpal, Indian journalist, publisher, novelist, and editor

—Alfred Lord Tennyson, Poet Laureate of Great Britain and Ireland

—Richard Thalheimer, founder, CEO, and chairman of The Sharper Image Corporation

—Mother Theresa, Roman Catholic nun and missionary

—Bennie Thompson, US congressman

—Robert G. Thompson, author

—Henry David Thoreau, author, poet, philosopher, abolitionist, and naturalist

—Samuel Thurm, senior vice president, US Association of National Advertisers

—Jeffry A. Timmons, professor of entrepreneurship

—Lily Tomlin, actress and comedian

—Matthew Toren, author, entrepreneur, and investor

—Robert Townsend, author

—Brian Tracy, author

—Harry Truman, US President

—Donald Trump, real estate developer and Republican Presidential nominee

—Fred Trump, real estate developer

—Harriet Tubman, abolitionist

—Sarah Tse, artist

—Ted Turner, founder of Turner Broadcasting and CNN

—Mark Twain, author and humorist

—Sun Tzu, Chinese general, military strategist, and philosopher

U

—Evelyn Underhill, English Anglo-Catholic writer and pacifist

—Carrie Underwood, singer-songwriter

V

—Martin Van Buren, US President

—Dick Van Dyke, actor and comedian

—Vincent Van Gogh, artist

—Cornelius Vanderbilt, industrialist

—Gloria Vanderbilt, fashion designer

—Gary Vaynerchuk, entrepreneur, investor, author, and Internet personality

—Queen Victoria, English royalty

—Gore Vidal, writer and public intellectual

— Vishnu, Hindu male deity

—Swami Vivekananda, Indian Hindu monk

—Roger Von Oech, speaker, author, and toy-maker

—Peter Voogd, media entrepreneur and author

W

—Denis Waitley, motivational speaker, writer, and consultant

—Izaak Walton, English writer

—Sam Walton, founder of Wal-Mart

—John Wanamaker, department-store magnate

—Eugene F. Ware, author

—George Washington, US President

—Thomas J. Watson, chairman of IBM

—Marlon Wayans, actor and comedian

—Jerry Weintraub, movie producer

—Jack Welch, chairman and CEO of GE

—Arsene Wenger, French football manager and former player

—John Wheeler, theoretical physicist

—Meg Whitman, chairman and CEO of Hewlett-Packard

—Meredith Whitney, financial analyst

—Eliot Wigginton, oral historian, folklorist, writer, and educator

—Oscar Wilde, Irish playwright, novelist, essayist, and poet

—George Will, newspaper columnist and political commentator

—Heather Williams, author

—Roy H. Williams, author and marketing consultant

—Oprah Winfrey, media mogul, television host, and actress

—Anna Wintour, *Vogue* magazine editor

—Susan Wojcicki, CEO of YouTube

—George Edward Woodberry, literary critic and poet

—John Wooden, legendary UCLA basketball coach

—Cornell Woolrich, novelist

—F.W. Woolworth, founder of five-and-dime chain

—Steve Wozniak, cofounder of Apple Inc.

—Steven Wright, comedian

—Steve Wynn, casino owner

Y

—Richard Yates, fiction writer

—Andrew Young, US Ambassador to U.N. and Atlanta mayor

—Jim Young, fictional character in the movie *Boiler Room*

—Muhammad Yunus, Nobel Peace Prize winner